Contents

Mankind and the Sea

1

It is true that in the wide and deep sea there are monsters that can swallow a person whole, and still others that will share their human feast in bits and pieces with other denizens of the dark waters. Some creatures drift aimlessly through the water, their presence undetected until they unleash their painful stinging power that can kill a person within minutes. On the beach, attractive shells that house living animals can shoot deadly darts into a hand or finger so swiftly that the victim may be unaware that he or she has been stung and has only a few hours to live. A diminutive octopus, looking harmless and pathetic in a tangle of seaweeds, can give a lethal nip with its parrotlike beak. The poison-bearing spine of a sea urchin, the razor-sharp edge of a pen shell—both can leave a throbbing wound that generally must be lanced in order to extract the broken pieces. Just brushing by a beautiful coral will slash skin, resulting in months of pain, itching, and aggravation.

Fish that are a gourmet's delight in one season can become deadly fare in another if caught during certain times of the year or in particular areas of the sea. Sometimes, primarily to demonstrate its productive value, some of the soupy sea is centrifuged to **5** concentrate its rich growth of plankton, and the thick sludge is then made into "burgers" or brewed into a broth. In most cases the results are indeed differently delicious and harmless. But beware! Unless those who prepared the plankton have been discriminating, they can quite innocently serve up lethal potions of some poisonous planktonic plant. Equally possible, the concoction may contain plants that are encased in siliceous shells, making the meal akin to serving cockleburs mixed with ground glass and quite capable of shredding a person's insides.

Yes, as you will discover in the following pages, the sea can indeed be dangerous—even killing. But since the beginning, mankind has always been challenged by the sea and its creatures. To primitive and superstitious people, this undersea world belonged wholly to the gods, but now mankind is beginning to uncover its secrets. Today nearly all governments and large universities operate oceanographic vessels from which studies of the sea and its life are made. One day there will be undersea farms, cities, and transportation.

But the underwater world is still largely unexplored; it is the earth's last frontier. Beneath the rolling waves is a world many times larger than the one we know. There are canyons that plunge to much greater depths than any on land. Undersea mountains that never break the water's surface are higher than Mount Everest. Ocean rivers a thousand times mightier than the Mississippi sweep through the seas. And there is actually only one ocean—a continuous body of water that surrounds the earth, occupying about sixty percent of the Northern Hemisphere and nearly ninety percent of the Southern Hemisphere.

To primitive peoples, the sea was the resting place of the sun and the moon. From its vast waters they harvested fish, clams, oysters, turtles, and other foods. On calm days the sea was often as blue as the sky, its smooth surface flecked white with **6** crumpled, weak waves. At these times the sea was good. But

also from the sea came the winds and rains of storms. In cloudy, stormy weather, the sea's surface turned a sullen gray-green. Mountainous waves rose like angry monsters eager to swallow all that lay in their path as they came crashing against the land.

Long before there were ships to sail the seas, man must have stood by the great waters and wondered from where they came and how far they stretched. He did not know there were other shores where the same sea washed the beaches and pounded the rocks. He knew only that a ribbon of shallow water separated him from the broad, deep sea, which was to him a mysterious power. To some people of early times, the sea contained many gods of both good and evil. To others, the sea was the home of just one god. The Greek's god of the sea was Oceanus. To the Romans, he became Neptune.

California barracuda ▲

At first people feared the sea, as they always fear the unknown. But the unknown also was a challenge to learn more about it. Perhaps the sea was first explored by accident, when a raft or a small boat used on calm, inland waters was swept out of sight of land with a frightened man aboard. But long before recorded history, people were purposely sailing boats farther toward the horizon. They had to know for themselves what it was like where the sea stopped.

In the small ships of early days, people did not dare to venture far onto the giant oceans. They sailed only the smaller seas, which soon became much-traveled trade routes. The Mediterranean Sea was sailed from shore to shore by the Greeks and the Phoenicians, for both were expert sailors. Eventually the bold ventured onto the big, blustery Atlantic. At first they kept land within sight, but these brave adventurers **9** nevertheless sailed the coasts of both Africa and Europe. The Greeks believed that the ocean was a great river flowing in a circle around the land that was the center of their flat world, but they were too cautious to try to prove this theory.

Ships large enough to sail the oceans were not built until the 1600s. Even then, however, mankind had only slight interest in the oceans themselves. They were simply watery barriers that lay between him and whatever riches could be found on the other side. The Vikings crossed the Atlantic five hundred years before Columbus, and it is known, too, that early Polynesian sailors coursed much of the great Pacific. But these sea voyagers left almost no records of their explorations. It was not until the voyages of Christopher Columbus, Vasco da Gama, Ponce de Leon, Vasco de Balboa, and Ferdinand

Magellan that people were convinced once and for all that a ship could sail west and return to the same port from the east. These men proved that the earth was round rather than flat.

The mystery and superstition about the sea began to be replaced by facts, and the truths were every bit as strange, marvelous, and unbelievable as the myths. Ships headed for every point on the compass, crossing the oceans primarily to discover new lands. But as time passed, people became more curious about the sea itself and its creatures. The surface conquered, mankind began to probe the ocean depths that some believed to harbor hideous monsters. The few fearsome beasts encountered along the shores and in the shallows were thought to be merely a small sampling of what lurked in deeper expanses of water.

▲ Spotted moray eel
◄ Shipwreck in Bermuda

No one knows who first looked at the world under the sea or why. It is most likely that it was in pursuit of a fish, or perhaps a lobster or an oyster. Some of the early people feasted on shellfish that live in water only twenty or thirty feet (6–9 m) deep, and that could only have been obtained by diving. Early civilizations used objects from the deep such as pearls and sponges. These divers told tempting tales of the sea's underwater beauty, its strange beasts, and its treasures. They lured others to explore this underwater world, too, and always the challenge was to go deeper and to stay longer.

12

▲ Coral

▲ Surgeonfish ▼ Shrimp

Depending on only the oxygen in his lungs, a diver cannot remain submerged for much longer than two minutes, even after intensive training and experience. By then he must be back at the surface to get more air. If he spends a minute of his time going down and a minute returning to the surface, he obviously cannot go very deep or linger long in looking around. To hurry themselves down, divers may hold a rock or some other kind of weight, and then let it go when they have gone as deep as they desire. A few divers have reached depths greater than one hundred and fifty feet (46 m) in this manner, but beyond a depth of one hundred feet (30 m) the pressure of the water becomes too great for human tolerance.

Greek sponge divers in ancient times learned to take precautions against the dangers of the depths. They filled their ears with oil and secured oil-soaked sponges over their ears as

Grouper ▲

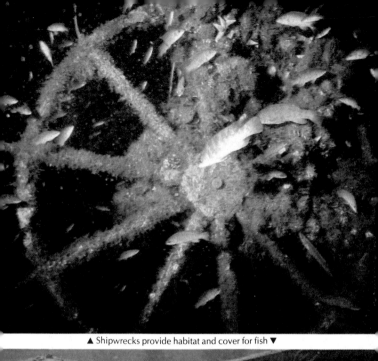

▲ Shipwrecks provide habitat and cover for fish ▼

well. Even so, the pressure of the depths was powerful and caused most divers eventually to become deaf. Due to the constant strain under which they worked and despite all efforts to keep themselves fit, these divers were not known for their long lives.

A variety of breathing-tube devices, or snorkels, were used for staying under water in the shallows. Probably the first were hollow reeds. Leonardo da Vinci sketched an underwater diving mask of a helmet that fit over the diver's head. A breathing tube attached to the front of the helmet led to the water's surface, where it was held up by a cork float. The entire helmet was studded with sharp spikes to protect the diver's head from fish or other creatures that might attack. Inside, the helmet was braced with hoops to prevent it from collapsing

16

Scorpionfish ▲

▲ Southern stingray ▼ Sea snake

against the diver's face. The diver looked out through two glass-covered eyeholes, and there were webbed flippers for the feet and hands to help the diver swim. This remarkable set-up and its ingenious creator were far ahead of their time.

Diving bells, which trap a supply of air under the surface, were also used many years ago. Alexander the Great is said to have found great pleasure watching fish under the Mediterranean Sea from beneath a diving bell. He told perhaps the tallest fish story of all times: he reported having seen one fish that took three days and three nights to pass by the window through which he was peering. In addition to having concocted a preposterous fish that only braced the tales about undersea behemoths, he greatly exaggerated about the length of his stay under water, for no diving bell was ever made that would trap air enough for such a long submergence. Diving bells were, nevertheless, a great step forward in allowing **18** people to see the underwater world.

White-tipped shark with pilot fish ▲

However, diving bells work effectively only in shallow water. The pressure of the trapped air under the bell is always the same as the pressure of the surrounding water. As the bell is pushed down deeper, the air is simply compressed, and the conditions inside the bell become uncomfortable.

In time, experimenters began to replenish the air inside by lowering inverted barrels and then turning them over, allowing the fresh air supply to escape into the bell. Still later, air was continuously pumped into the bell from a bellows at the surface. This not only replenished the oxygen but also helped to balance the pressure.

Eventually the diving bells were supplied with compressed air so that deeper descents could be made. In some diving bells the divers stood on platforms attached to the inside. Thus the bell would not have to rest directly on the bottom in order to support the diver. Working from the platforms, with their heads in the trapped-air space, divers could use hooks and long poles to reach whatever they wished. This permitted them to lift items from the decks of sunken ships in salvage chores and to closely examine the sea creatures they found.

Diving bells did not allow free movement under the sea, however, so special diving suits were built in which air was supplied through a hose to the helmet. Now divers could walk about on the ocean bottom, a great advantage over the diving bells, but could still only move the length of the air hose, the lifeline to the surface. But the diver was restricted to moving about only on the bottom because of the weighted shoes and belts he wore to keep himself submerged.

Even in diving suits, divers were still limited to exploration on the continental shelf, in water less than six hundred feet (183 m) deep. They were not able to probe greater depths of the sea because beyond six hundred feet, air must be supplied under more pressure. This causes some of the free nitrogen in the air to be taken into the diver's blood, and as he then comes to the surface, the nitrogen is released. Divers must come up **19**

from the depths slowly so that their return to normal atmospheric pressure is not abrupt and the nitrogen can escape the blood through their lungs. A return that is too rapid causes nitrogen to be released at an accelerated rate, which then forms bubbles in the blood. These bubbles cause severe pains, known as "the bends," and death may even be the result.

Diving suits are being modernized, however. The problem of discomfort from working in cold water is being solved with nuclear-heated suits. In the past, the extreme coldness of deep water has been a major factor limiting the length of time that a diver could stay beneath the surface.

Aqualungs, invented in 1943 by Jacques Cousteau and Emil Gagnam, have made it possible for thousands of people to prowl in shallow waters. Few divers using these underwater lungs, or self-contained underwater breathing devices (scuba), **20** go deeper than three hundred feet (91 m), though it is possible

Gray nurse shark ▲

to go to depths of five hundred feet (152 m). But even in the shallowest waters, people are seeing the sea as it has never been seen before. Some hurry themselves along with underwater scooters, small motorized units that swiftly transport the diver from place to place, which permit the diver to conserve his energy for probing and examining.

One of the most exciting recent ideas has been the possibility of developing a membrane that will allow humans to breathe underwater like a fish. Oxygen in the water passes through the membrane, while water remains on the other side. If this sort of device works as well as expected, divers can stay submerged for as long as they wish in depths where the pressure permits. But an even more astonishing discovery is that a person may be able to breathe underwater even without a membrane if his lungs are flooded with water containing a high concentration of oxygen. At low pressures near the sur-

face, water does not contain enough oxygen for a human being's needs, but experiments with laboratory animals have demonstrated that the lungs of warm-blooded animals can utilize oxygen directly from the water if it is available in large enough amounts.

Another experiment was conducted with a man in which one lung was flooded with water under high enough pressure to hold large amounts of oxygen. This lung then functioned like a fish's gill. In this kind of underwater breathing, for example, there will not be a problem with nitrogen, for the water does not carry nitrogen in solution. Divers will be able to surface as rapidly as they wish without having to endure the long decompression period.

Some scientists speculate that this might account for the ability of air-breathing whales to remain underwater for such **22** long periods. They may go deep enough to take water directly into their lungs, and in such cases their "spouts" actually clear water from their lungs rather than a condensation of warm, moist air, which is the usual explanation.

When will people be able to explore the sea like fish or whales? Of course, no one knows exactly—but by these various means, the world beneath the waves is steadily being conquered by those with questioning minds and with courage.

Mankind's historic step in deep-sea exploration came in the early 1930s with the invention of the bathysphere. It consisted of a hollow steel sphere with walls 1½ inches (3.8 cm) thick and quartz windows 3 inches (7.6 cm) thick. Oxygen was supplied from cylinders carried inside the bathysphere, and the carbon dioxide and moisture released in breathing were absorbed by chemicals. A searchlight outside the sphere scanned the dark sea as the vessel was lowered on a steel cable from a ship at the surface.

In the bathysphere, biologist William Beebe descended into the sea off Bermuda to a depth of more than half a mile. He gave the world the first accurate and detailed descriptions of the strange creatures of the deep sea. What he discovered was that instead of becoming more monstrous, as people generally believed, the creatures became increasingly smaller—the pressure and food scarcity limiting their size to scant dimensions. And fortunately, too, for these small beasts are indeed the most frightening in appearance of all animals. Their weaponry for luring and seizing prey is unequalled by any others. Most of these creatures have stomachs so stretchable that they can swallow animals larger than themselves.

In 1960, mankind took another landmark step in deep-sea exploration and for the first time saw the deepest part of the ocean. The trip to the bottom was in the United States Navy's *Trieste,* an unusual vessel called a bathyscaphe. The two men who made the descent were cramped into a steel sphere about 6½ feet (1.8 m) in diameter centered on the underside of a 50-foot (15.2-m) sausage-shaped tank filled with more than **23**

Inspection of bathyscape Trieste's sphere ▲

35,000 gallons (133,000 l) of gasoline. Gasoline was chosen because it is not greatly affected by pressure in the depths. Since gasoline is lighter than water, the tank lifted the vessel, just as a lighter-than-air gas lifts a dirigible. The *Trieste* is, in fact, often referred to as an "underwater balloon." To carry the *Trieste* down, ten tons (9 m tons) of iron were held to its underside by electromagnets.

On its memorable voyage to the bottom of the Challenger Deep in January, 1960, the *Trieste* drifted down, down, down. **24** Nearly five hours after leaving the surface, the strange vessel

Bathyscaphe being made ready for the sea ▲

finally settled on the bottom, nearly seven miles (10 km) below the surface in the Mariana Trench off Guam.

More than 200,000 tons of pressure per square inch (6.5 sq cm) pushed in on the 3½-inch (9.3-cm) thick steel walls of the sphere. Yet as they peered through their thick plastic windows, held firmly in place by the pressure of the water pushing in from the outside, the two men aboard the *Trieste* saw a flounderlike fish resting on the bottom nearby. A shrimp scurried past and disappeared in the darkness. An amazing discovery had been made: even in the deepest spot of the sea there are living things.

The *Trieste* stayed on the bottom only about twenty minutes. Then the electromagnets were turned off to release the tons of iron, and the vessel slowly rose to the surface, its trip back taking slightly more than three hours. At last a centuries-old dream had been realized.

The *Trieste* had overcome a major disadvantage of Beebe's bathysphere: it did not have a cable connection to the surface that limited the depth and movability of the vessel. But the *Trieste* could not move about with total freedom either. This can only be done in a movable vessel—a submarine.

Submarines move like fish in the quiet darkness of the sea, escaping the storms and rough waves at the surface by traveling far below. Because they are hidden from sight, they have been especially important for military reasons and were developed, in fact, mainly for use in war. But while they were born out of warfare, their most important role now is in helping scientists explore the underwater world. Research submarines are mostly small vessels that carry crews of from two to a dozen. Though many submarines are designed for work in the shallow waters of the continental shelves, some can go deep—to 20,000 feet (7,000 m) or more. They are amply supplied with viewing windows and searchlights, and they have clawlike arms for picking up objects from the bottom. Some can remain underwater for more than two days, and **25**

▼Ocean floor as viewed by Trieste I ▲ Trieste submerging off the Boston coast

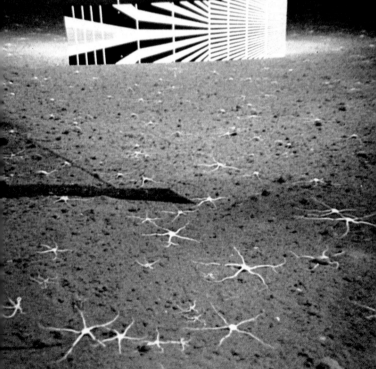

several permit divers to leave and reenter them underwater.

Within a few years, technologists expect to have developed vessels that will travel under the sea at speeds of one hundred miles (160 km) per hour. These undersea vessels will be used primarily to haul cargoes. Below the surface they will be assured of safe passage from storms and polar ice, and will not have to overcome friction as do surface ships. Undersea traffic control centers will be necessary near ports as the number of these vessels increases. Tourists will be thrilled by undersea excursions giving them close looks at "inner space" and all its inhabitants.

And so it has come to pass that with each year and in many ways mankind's intimacy with the sea has increased. Advanced technology now permits almost anyone to invade the sea as it has never before been possible and to meet its creatures in their environment. The great increase in the world's population means that more and more people are at seashores and onto or into the waters either for work or for recreation. For many people the sea and its creatures are fearsome, mainly because they are encountering the unknown. Caution is wise, for the sea does contain dangers of many sorts. But the sea is really less dangerous to mankind than the land with its rats, lice, fleas, poisonous snakes, poisonous plants, epidemic diseases, and other natural scourges. Even these, which are far greater in magnitude than the dangers of the sea, are diminutive compared to mankind's own contrivances—such as automobiles and planes.

The greatest danger to people in their encounters with the sea is panic—the loss of rationality. In the pages that follow, only the dangerous animals of the sea are described, a necessary focus but one that may make it appear that the sea is wholly formidable. Do not be misled! With caution and common sense as guides, the sea is safe and enjoyable. Use this book only as a guide to help you in avoiding those unlikely experiences that might be dangerous. **27**

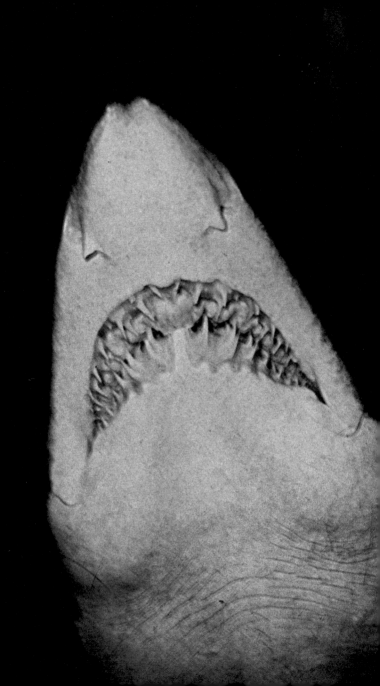

Sharks 2

Some sharks are harmless, either ill-equipped or not inclined to give damaging bites. Others are among the most fearsome creatures of the sea, capable of biting off a person's arm or leg or even big enough to swallow him whole. Every year the statistical evidence indicting sharks as killers becomes greater. This is partly because today more accurate records are being kept, but it is also true that many more people are venturing into the sea to swim or dive. In doing so they are entering the world of sharks and either intentionally or unwittingly tempting and taunting these primitive beasts that respond instinctively with their razor-sharp teeth to protect themselves and their territory. About a third of all shark attacks on people are fatal. In most attacks, however, the shark makes a single bite and then departs. In these instances it seems apparent that the shark did not have a meal in mind.

In 1958, the American Institute of Biological Sciences formed the Shark Research Panel to keep records of shark attacks throughout the world. Information is collected on the location and date of the attack, the name and age of the victim, the extent of the injury or whether the attack was fatal, the kind of shark, and whether the incident was **29**

◀ Sand tiger shark

provoked. The purpose of this Shark Attack File is not just to have a collection of data but to learn about the behavior of sharks and what triggers their attacks. By assembling this information, the Shark Research Panel hopes to be able to lower the number of attacks in the future. To date, two important factors stand out in the statistics: the greatest number of attacks occur during those months when the largest number of people go to the beaches to swim and hence are exposed to possible attacks; and the attacks are most numerous when the visibility is lowest, as on cloudy days, after dark or at dusk, and in murky water.

It is also evident, *Jaws* to the contrary, that sharks are much maligned by exaggerated stories. While they are indeed dangerous and should never be underestimated or trusted, it is really most miraculous that the actual number of attacks is so few. If sharks were, in fact, as wholly charged with man-eating instincts as the tales about them would have it, no one would dare put a foot in the sea or even set out in a small boat. The sharks *are* there—in far greater numbers than people would ever believe—but they are for the most part not especially interested in humans. Even the largest sharks ordinarily shy away from such encounters.

Except for man, sharks have virtually no enemies. Killer whales can subdue sharks of any size, it's true, but they do not make a special effort to hunt them. Other porpoises at times seem to derive pleasure in exhibiting their speed and dexterity by tossing sharks about, but they are not shark hunters. There is evidence, too, that sharks have lost in battles with giant squids and other animals, but sharks are generally left alone in the sea. Because they are cannibalistic, sharks are more dangerous to themselves than are other animals. Their role in nature is as scavenger-predators that clean up the dead and the near-dying, nature's assurance that only the quick and alert survive to produce more of their kind.

30   Sharks belong to an ancient group of fishes, the Chondrichthyes, that has existed for more than three hundred million years but is represented today by only some two hundred and fifty species. They were never abundant, however, because their successful form did not foster diversity in their line of development. They represent a sort of evolutionary "blind alley" and have been described by some scientists as the most nearly perfect of all the predators, because of their torpedo-shaped bodies, powerful jaws and sharp teeth, and seemingly insatiable appetites. One of the extinct sharks was the largest fish ever to have lived. It measured as much as 100 feet (30.5 m) long, and its mouth was so large that a full-grown man could have stood in its jaws. Its triangular teeth were 4 inches (10 cm) high. The largest shark alive today—and still the largest of all fish—is the whale shark *(Rhincodon typus)*, which may reach a length of 60 feet (18.3 m) and weigh as much as 15 tons (13.5 m tons). But this giant is a plankton feeder, harmless to man except for accidental injuries caused

▲ Dorsal fin of a great white shark

by the lashing of its monstrous tail. A whale shark does have teeth—more than 7,000, in fact—but none is more than an eighth of an inch (3 mm) high. These teeth help form the plankton trap with which the big shark gets its meals by sieving tiny creatures from the water. The smallest is the dwarf shark (*Squaliolus laticaudus*), less than a foot long when full grown.

General Anatomy

Sharks—and also rays, which belong to same group—have skeletons of cartilage rather than bone. This is the same sort of tough, flexible material of which your nose is made. Cartilage is much lighter in weight than is bone and thus helps the shark in swimming. Some sharks have spindle-shaped bodies and are swift swimmers—among the fastest animals in the sea. They can swim backward nearly as fast as they can move forward, but they cannot stop or turn as well as can the more maneuverable bony fishes (Osteichthyes) that account for nearly all of our present-day species of fish. Other sharks are sluggish, spending most of their time lying on the bottom. Unlike the more advanced bony fishes, the sharks do not have a swim bladder, which serves as a hydrostatic organ so that fish can adjust to various depths and stay in balance. Unless a shark keeps in motion, it will sink. Sharks do get some degree of buoyancy from the large amount of oil in their liver (in most, equaling about a fourth their total body weight). The lack of a gas-filled bladder enables them to change depths without danger of the bladder exploding, as it sometimes does in bony fishes when they are brought up from the depths too quickly.

Sharks have several gill slits on each side rather than a single covered opening as do bony fishes. Most sharks also have a spiracle, or hole, just behind each eye. In breathing, water enters this hole (rather than the mouth as in bony fishes), and then passes over the gills. This is another important reason why sharks must swim constantly, for they cannot pump water **32** over their gills by opening and shutting their mouth. The

water, bearing oxygen for their gills, moves into the spiracle only when the shark moves. The patrolling movements of a shark, therefore, do not necessarily mean that it is on the prowl for food. It is simply breathing and keeping itself afloat.

A number of species of sharks do occur in brackish and even freshwaters, but all sharks are basically marine animals, their departure from the sea strictly secondary. Because of their problem with buoyancy and breathing, they have difficulty in being comfortable out of saltwater.

Typically a shark's tail has a much larger upper than lower lobe, the exceptions being sharks that live in the open sea. But even in these sharks the spine extends into the upper tail lobe also, giving it support and supplying the power for swimming. The tail is the shark's driving force, with the fins being used only for stabilization. The fins are covered with the same thick, tough skin that covers the body—rather than consisting of spiny and soft rays with webs between them as in bony fishes. The fins are rigid and cannot be folded against the body. In the fast swimmers, the first dorsal fin is located far forward on the body and is the principal stabilizer.

A typical shark's scales, called placoid, are similar in their structure to tiny teeth, complete with enamel, dentine, and a pulp cavity. They are small and scattered over the body, occurring more abundantly in some sharks than in others. But **33**

▲ White-tipped shark

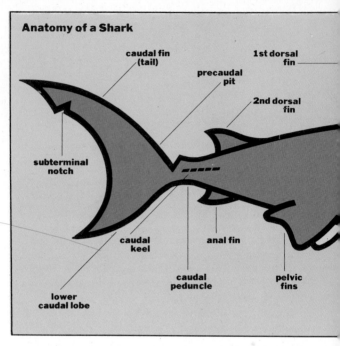

Anatomy of a Shark

caudal fin (tail)

precaudal pit

1st dorsal fin

2nd dorsal fin

subterminal notch

caudal keel

anal fin

lower caudal lobe

caudal peduncle

pelvic fins

some are large enough to cut deeply if a shark is handled or even rubbed against. This unusual skin is known commercially as shagreen.

The shark's teeth, which are identical in structure to the scales, are not rooted in its jaws but fit almost loosely in a tough membrane just inside the jaws. Some sharks have flattened teeth for crushing shells. Plankton eaters such as giant whale and basking sharks have tiny teeth. The teeth of carnivorous sharks are pointed and either slim or broadly triangular. Most of these sharks have teeth with cutting edges as sharp as razor blades, and some teeth even have serrated edges. The most fearsome of these sharp-toothed sharks may have as many as a thousand teeth in a dozen or more rows. Only one row is functional at a time, but when a tooth is broken, worn, or lost, it is quickly replaced. Some sharks have two kinds of

teeth: sharp, pointed ones at the front of the mouth, and flat,

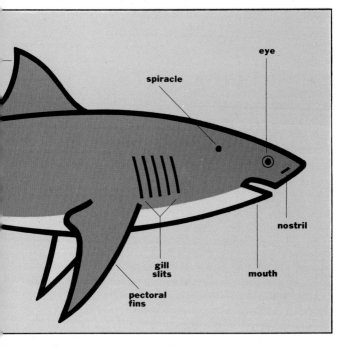

spiracle

eye

nostril

gill
slits

mouth

pectoral
fins

crushing teeth at the rear. The shape of a shark's tooth is so
characteristic that a species can be identified by the pattern of
the wound it makes. Sometimes the mark of a single tooth is a
sufficient clue.

The shark's mouth opens under its snout, and depending on
the size and position of its prey, a shark may turn on its side or
even upside down to make its bite. (In literature, it is often said
that a shark must turn over in order to bite, but this upside-
down position is actually not essential.) When biting, some
sharks open their mouth so wide that their snout becomes
nearly perpendicular and their teeth stand out almost straight
in front. The bite wounds are typically half-moon shaped, and
the deep cuts are made as the shark shakes its head back and
forth and slashes with its teeth. This is done with such great
speed that a shark is capable of cutting its prey in two within a
matter of seconds.

Intelligence and Senses

In terms of intelligence or ability to learn or remember, sharks do not have well-developed brains. Nature has programmed them nearly to perfection for their predatory and scavenging role in the sea, however. Some of the sensory portions of their nervous systems are highly specialized. They have a superior sense of smell, for example, enabling them to detect and then zero in on mere traces of odors such as blood, sometimes coming from as far as a quarter of a mile away with deadly accuracy. As it is "homing," a shark will turn its head from side to side time and again to make certain it is still precisely on target. In experiments in which one of the nostrils is plugged, the shark makes its approach by circling, the open nostril always toward the source of the odor. If both nostrils are plugged, the shark cannot find the odor source at all. Roughly two-thirds of a shark's brain consists of its olfactory lobes that control its sense of smell. Its nostrils are located just in front of the mouth and at the tip of the snout.

Sense organs of taste are located in pits scattered over the shark's entire body, and so putting a morsel of food near a shark's tail may excite the beast into a frenzy. With its taste organs, a shark can apparently distinguish the kind of food— that is, whether it is a fish, turtle, etc.

Sharks also have highly sensitive lateral lines (sensory organs in visible lines down each side of the body) with which they can detect movements in the water or even low-frequency vibrations. They also have internal "ears," consisting of a fluid-filled sac attached to the skull. In experiments, sharks learn to respond to a ringing bell or some similar noise as a signal for feeding time. A shark's senses—particularly of smell but also of taste and hearing—are especially useful to them in locating and then homing in on food.

A shark's vision is good but is evidently not exceptional. It is nearsighted, which is typical of aquatic animals, but it can see under water better than a human. Vision is not of great impor-

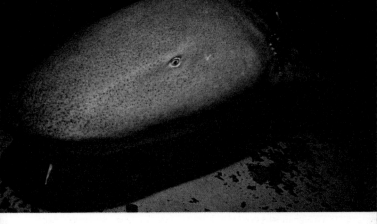

tance to sharks in finding their food, as most of them hunt at night. The shark's sense of pain is very poorly developed—so much so that in their feeding frenzies a shark may literally be eaten in half by its shark companions and still continue to feed ravenously itself. It may even eat parts of its own body that have been detached without showing signs of discomfort.

Reproduction

All sharks reproduce by internal fertilization. The male is equipped with a pair of claspers on his pelvic fins, and these are inserted into the female to transfer sperm to her ovaries. A male of one species is incapable of mating with a female of another species, however, as the claspers do not fit properly to open the oviduct for fertilization. This type of fertilization does occur in some of the bony fishes but is rare.

Some sharks are oviparous—that is, they lay eggs that hatch in the water. Each egg is enclosed in a leathery capsule, which in some species has long tendrils at the edges that wrap around seaweeds or other objects for anchorage. After the eggs hatch, the empty cases float in the sea and are often cast onto beaches. Collectors call them ''mermaids' purses.''

Most sharks are ovoviviparous, retaining the eggs inside **37**

▲ Nurse shark

their bodies until they hatch. As in other animals, they generally produce fewer young than do those that lay eggs, but a much smaller percentage of the laid eggs hatch and survive. Development inside the mother's body has distinct survival advantages.

Still other sharks are viviparous, the embryos nourished inside the mother's body through a primitive placenta similar to that in mammals. The young of these sharks may be astonishingly large at birth—up to one-fourth as long as the mother. They are completely equipped for independent existence at birth. Researchers have even been bitten by unborn sharks still encased in the embryonic sac inside their mother. Young sharks are called pups.

Value of Sharks
Sharks do have their worth. In addition to their important role in nature as predators and as scavengers, many kinds of sharks are valued commercially and also provide sport for anglers. For years the coarse skin of sharks, known in industry as shagreen, was one of the primary abrasives used in smoothing wood to a satiny finish. In days gone by, warriors of primitive tribes wrapped the handles of their knives and swords with shagreen so they could keep a firm grip on them. In most parts of the world, shagreen has now been replaced with other substances, but it can still be bought in parts of Africa and other regions largely untouched by modern technology. With the denticles removed, sharkskin is processed to make a highly durable leather for belts, shoes, and other items. Since ancient times, too, the sharp teeth of sharks have been used to make saws, to tip arrows or other weapons, and to provide keen edges for shaving or thinning hair. The teeth have also been used to make necklaces and other kinds of jewelry, and they have been ground up as an additive to some medicines.

Until the late 1940s, sharks were a major source of vitamin
A, which is now produced synthetically and less expensively

in laboratories. Sometimes the shark oil was marketed as cod liver oil. Shark oil is still used in many countries, of course, and in addition to serving as a source of vitamin A, it is utilized in tanning leather and making soap. The amount of oil derived from a single shark's huge liver can be substantial.

The greatest use of sharks is as food, the commercial harvest exceeding a billion pounds annually. Some sharks are poisonous if not prepared properly (see page 133), but others are ranked among the finest delicacies of the seas. One of the prized dishes of the Orient is sharkfin soup. Prepared by experienced cooks and from fresh fins, it may require four or five days to produce sharkfin soup that satisfies a perfectionistic Chinese cook. One of the biggest users of sharks for food is Japan, and much of the catch is processed to make kamaboko—a kind of fish cake. Sharks are also popular in many European countries, and they are canned or smoked as well as being sold fresh. The unused portions of the sharks are converted into a meal that is fed to livestock so that the contribution of the catch is total. Sharks can also be utilized in making the protein-rich concentrate that is heralded by some authorities as a major help in adding inexpensively to the diets of protein-starved peoples (see page 127).

Of the many kinds of sharks, dogfish (*Squalus acanthias* and others) are the most utilized. Often they are sold in markets as "grayfish," or sometimes—and illegally so—they are passed off as completely different species. Dogfish are harvested because of their great abundance and the ease with which they **39**

▲ Blue shark

can be netted in inshore waters. Food authorities confirm that the dogfish is indeed an excellent source of protein, actually superior pound for pound to oysters, mackerels, or even milk and eggs. But there is a long-standing prejudice that keeps the utilization of sharks at a low level in many countries. People are generally reticent about eating animals that are known also to eat people. The shark taboo is ancient, however. In the Bible, people are warned not to eat any of the "scaleless" creatures of the sea. This, of course, includes sharks.

Since earliest times, the catching of sharks has challenged the most daring of men. With harpoons, snares, guns, giant hooks and chains, men have set out to best these beasts of the sea. Fishermen often hook sharks by accident, the sharks taking baits intended for other kinds of fish. Sharks also make pests of themselves by taking hooked dolphins, tunas, or other sport fish before they can can be boated, and still other sharks foul the nets of commercial fishermen.

But for some sport fishermen, sharks offer unsurpassable thrills. The sport of shark fishing can become such a mania that some anglers go after no other kind of fish, and there are even fishing clubs that specialize exclusively in catching sharks. The ranking of sharks as big game fish dates back half a century when Zane Grey began tackling the monsters in Australian waters. The species challenging him most was the mako. A hooked mako is comparable to or surpasses a marlin, swordfish, tarpon, or any other big game fish in aerial acrobatics—a giant torpedo that leaps stiffly and nearly verti- cally from the water time after time, often dangerously close to or even over the boat. But while the mako is certainly the most spectacular catch, other species of sharks also offer excite- ment to rod-and-reel fishermen. The International Game Fish Association keeps records of six other species in addition to the mako, recognizing all of them as superior game fish. In their current all-tackle records, these are the top weights of the **40** sharks and the location of the catch:

Blue Shark, *410 lbs. (186 kg), Rockport,*
Massachusetts, 1960, plus another of identical weight
caught in the same area in 1967
Great White Shark, *2,664 lbs. (1,208 kg), Ceduna,*
South Australia, 1959 (Note: a new record of
3,388 lbs (1,537 kg) is pending acceptance
by the IGFA.)
Hammerhead Shark, *703 lbs. (319 kg),*
Jacksonville, Florida, 1975
Porbeagle Shark, *430 lbs. (195 kg),*
Channel Islands, England, 1969
Mako Shark, *1,061 lbs. (481 kg), Mayor Island,*
New Zealand, 1970
Thresher Shark, *739 lbs. (337 kg), Tutkaka,*
New Zealand, 1975
Tiger Shark, *1,780 lbs. (812 kg), Cherry Grove,*
South Carolina, 1964

It is interesting that all of these records are recent, evidence
that there is no shortage of big sharks in the seas.

How to Avoid Shark Bites
Much myth and misinformation surrounds sharks. As a group,
sharks are not all bloodthirsty beasts with a vendetta against
mankind. Fewer than ten percent of all species of sharks are
known definitely to be dangerous to humans, but that is a
sufficient number—particularly when you are not given an
opportunity to check their credentials—to make it important
to give all sharks complete respect. In most parts of the world
the chances of being attacked by a shark are extremely slim,
but it is wise to be cautious wherever you are in the sea and to
avoid all sharks no matter what their size is or what their
disposition seems to be. Sharks have different moods, too, and
much may depend on whether the shark has had a recent meal
or is having hunger pangs. A shark's behavior is unpredictable.

If you do encounter a shark, resist any temptation you may
have to poke at it, even if it is a small one and you are in
shallow water. Remember, sharks have a very low intelligence. Do not trust them. Always heed shark warnings on **41**

beaches and stay out of the water at those times. Never go in water where sharks are suspected, and always swim with a companion. Do not swim at night or in murky water where both you and the shark might have difficulty seeing.

If you are skin diving and spear a fish, get it out of the water immediately. If you tow it, you and your fish both become shark bait—and especially if there is any blood in the water. Sharks are quick and unerring in finding the source of blood, which to them means a meal.

There have been all sorts of suggestions on how to discourage sharks. Some work—but not always. A shark that plans to attack will usually circle you one or several times, getting increasingly close. Do not panic. Move steadily but not frantically to get out of the water while at the same time preparing to take action if the shark persists in coming closer. Sometimes a sudden release of bubbles will send an inquisitive shark on its way. Some divers have reported that charging the shark will call its bluff. Others shout underwater, for sharks appear to be extremely sensitive to vibrations. If the shark comes within reach, hit it on the nose with a speargun or whatever you might be carrying. (Avoid using your hand, for remember, its scales are as sharp as its teeth.) If the beast is only being intimately inquisitive, this could suffice to kill its curiosity.

If it is absolutely necessary for you to be in waters where there are sharks, you can get shark repellents that discourage their approach or special guns to dispatch the beasts if they persist in bothering you.

Statistics show that the number of people attacked by sharks every year is minimal in comparison to most other kinds of hazards. You are much safer in the sea than riding in an automobile, for example. But no one wants to risk the chance of being one of those few who are attacked. The idea is chilling, particularly the thought of being eaten alive.

The sharks described on the following pages are those that
have at least some record of attacking humans. This does not

exclude the possibility of attacks by other species as man continues to invade the sharks' watery world. The sharks are listed here in phylogenetic order—from the most primitive to the most advanced.

Gray Nurse Shark *(Carcharias arenarius)*

The gray nurse shark is inappropriately named because it is brown rather than gray and also because its nasty disposition is discrediting to nurses. It roams warm seas throughout the world but occurs in greatest abundance in the coastal and estuarine waters of Australia and southern Africa. In both areas it is ranked as the most dangerous of the sharks, and records hold it responsible for the greatest number of attacks in shallow waters. The gray nurse shark reaches a length of 15 feet (4.6 m), and its mouth houses slim, back-curved teeth with which it can cut a human in two. Sometimes it appears in large numbers in beach areas, chasing schools of fish but devouring whatever comes in its path.

Sand Tiger or Sand Shark *(Carcharias taurus)*

Closely related to the gray nurse shark (sometimes considered to be the same species, in fact), the sand tiger is found most abundantly in the Atlantic off the coasts of North America and Europe but ranges widely throughout the world. The sand tiger rarely exceeds a length of six feet (1.8 m) but has been recorded to 10½ feet (3.2 m). It is rather sluggish. Generally it is not feared and is even considered harmless. Authorities point out, however, that this shark does have a vicious, unpredicta- **43**

▲ Gray nurse shark

ble disposition and that in some parts of the world, particularly off the coast of southeastern Asia, it attacks with regularity. Several unprovoked attacks have also been recorded off the east coast of the United States, where this shark sometimes appears in large numbers. It has sharp, stilettolike teeth, and when fishermen catch it accidentally in their nets, the sand tiger (so named because of the dark stripe down its back and the dark brown spots on its sides) is quick to bite in self-defense if it does not rip the nets and escape before being hauled in. Its dangerousness is minimized only by its rather small size, those most commonly caught only about three feet (90 cm) long. Sand tigers are also frequently taken accidentally on hook and line, but they are not good battlers. The sand tiger is one of the treacherous or untrustworthy sharks, definitely dangerous despite its long-standing reputation to the contrary.

Great White Shark (Carcharodon carcharias)
This giant is the most infamous of all the sharks, as testified by two other names by which it is widely known: man-eating shark and white death. The great white shark was the principal character in Peter Benchley's best-selling novel Jaws. This big shark averages about ten feet (3 m) in length but may get considerably larger. A great white shark 36½ feet (11.1 m) long was caught off Australia. This monster was not weighed. But a 21-footer (6.4 m) weighed 7,000 pounds (4,173 kg), its liver alone accounting for more than 1,000 pounds (454 kg). A 15-footer (4.6 m) weighed 2,500 pounds (1,135 kg). The largest fish ever caught on rod and reel, taken in Australian waters in April, 1976, was a great white shark that weighed 3,388 pounds (1,537 kg) and was 16 feet (4.9 m) long. A Brisbane angler battled the monster for almost five hours before it was subdued.

This behemoth is not common anywhere and is usually seen only in the open sea where it may bask at the surface or cruise
swiftly, its huge dorsal fin cutting the water like a knife. It is

known also to dive to depths of half a mile or more. Occasionally the great white shark does come close to shore, appearing most regularly off the coast of Australia and sometimes in quite shallow water.

Though heavy-bodied, it is nevertheless swift and streamlined. At the base of each of its large pectoral fins is an identifying black spot. Unlike most sharks, its upper and lower tail lobes are nearly equal in size. On each side of the caudal peduncle (the narrowed stalklike portion connecting the tail to the body) is a stiff keel that serves as a stabilizer. The teeth are broadly triangular with serrated edges and can be as long as two inches (5 cm). Large sharks—more than ten feet long—are grayish white, a dull lead color; smaller ones are dark gray. All ages and sizes are glistening white on the belly.

The great white shark has a voracious appetite and will attack and eat almost anything that moves. Typically it gulps down its meals whole—including humans. It has been known to attack boats fearlessly. The stomachs of dead white sharks have revealed meals of sea turtles, other sharks up to six feet (1.8 m) long, big fish, and even sea lions. To picture the great white shark as a beast wholly bent on destruction is incorrect, however. Some divers who have encountered these monsters **45**

▲ Great white shark

report that some of them seem surprisingly wary and unapproachable. Their boldness apparently depends on the emptiness of their stomach, which is big enough to make almost anything a potential meal.

Mako Shark *(Isurus oxyrinchus)*

Found in the Atlantic from temperate to tropical waters, the mako shark is the fastest of its clan. It is also noted for its spectacular leaps that make it a favorite with sport fishermen. It seems to be tireless in its fights and makes jump after jump in trying to free itself from hook and line. Though it averages less than six feet (1.8 m) in length and does not ordinarily weigh more than 200 pounds (91 kg), the mako is known to exceed 12 feet (3.6 m) and to weigh as much as 1,200 pounds (544 kg). The record caught on rod and reel weighed 1,061 pounds (481.3 kg) and was taken off New Zealand in 1970.

The mako is one of the most dangerous sharks in the seas,

sometimes attacking fishermen's boats or taking their hooked catches. It is reported to hunt specifically for big swordfish, which are said to have few other enemies in the seas. Makos have been killed with swordfish weighing more than a hundred pounds and still completely intact inside the shark's stomach. Larger swordfish may require several bites before they can be swallowed, but the mako downs most meals whole.

Because the mako is a pelagic species, it is not a threat in shallow waters or along beaches. Like other fishes of the open sea, it is dark blue above and lighter below. In many respects, the mako resembles the great white shark but is a swifter swimmer. Its teeth are much more slender and are smooth-edged. The lobes of its tail are equal in size, and there is a strong stabilizing keel on each side of the caudal peduncle. Other names for the mako are bonito shark, sharp-nosed shark, and mackerel shark.

47

▲ Mako shark

Porbeagle Shark and
Salmon Shark *(Lamna nasus* and *Lamna ditropis)*
The porbeagle shark lives in temperate to cool waters (below 60° F, 15° C) in the Atlantic, and the closely related salmon shark occupies the same habitat in the Pacific. They are members of the same family as the great white and the mako, and like them, they are fierce predators, feeding on mackerels and other swift-swimming fishes. Like the mako, they have slender, smooth-edged teeth for holding prey. These sharks average about five feet (1.5 m) in length, but occasional individuals may attain a length of ten feet (3 m) or more. They have thick bodies but are swift swimmers, though not as fast as the mako. Neither the porbeagle nor the salmon shark has an authenticated record in recent times of attacks on humans, but both are equipped with the weaponry to be dangerous.

Atlantic Nurse Shark *(Ginglymostoma cirratum)*
This sluggish shark, averaging five feet (1.5 m) in length although it can be twice as long, is abundant in shallow, warm Atlantic waters from North Carolina to Brazil and also off the coast of Africa. Sometimes it strays as far north as New York, and it appears from time to time in the Gulf of Mexico. It is a bottom dweller, with two sensory barbels, or ''whiskers,'' hanging under its snout. Its tail has almost no lower lobe.

Off the coast of the United States the fearless Atlantic nurse shark is the most commonly encountered of all sharks. It usually makes little or no attempt to bite, seeming to be wholly inoffensive. But by nature it will protect itself if molested, and the practice by some foolish people of holding onto its pectoral fins or its tail to be given an exciting ride may also result in a bite. Literally dozens of bites have been credited to this shark in recent years, most of them provoked by people. The shark has small teeth but powerful jaws, which hold on tenaciously. **48** Adults are grayish brown; the pups have black spots.

▲ Nurse shark with remora ▼ Spotted wobbegong

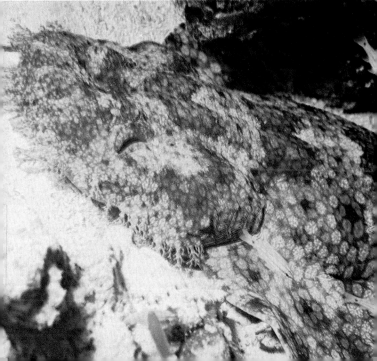

Spotted Wobbegong *(Orectolobus maculatus)*

Several species of sharks common in Indo-Pacific waters and most abundant off the Australian coasts are known collectively as wobbegongs. Though they belong to the same family as the drab Atlantic nurse shark, wobbegongs are the most colorful of all the sharks in the seas. The spotted wobbegong, for example, is decorated with numerous yellowish eyespots over its brown body and has a dozen or more fleshy barbels on its snout, as do other members of the family. A closely related species *(Stegostoma fasciatum)* is striped like a zebra. The attractive hides of these sharks are often used for leather. The varied colors and mottled patterns of these sharks provide camouflage when they are lying in seaweeds or among rocks in shallow water waiting for prey to venture near. Wobbegongs average less than five feet (1.5 m) in length, but the zebra shark may exceed ten feet (3 m). Unlike the Atlantic nurse shark, which is ovoviviparous (or retains its eggs inside its body until they hatch), the wobbegongs lay eggs, each in a long, leathery capsule with tendrils that anchor it to objects on the bottom.

Like the Atlantic nurse shark, the wobbegongs are not ordinarily aggressive, but a few cases of unprovoked attacks have been reported. Most of the attacks occur when a wobbegong is unintentionally stepped on by a wader or when a shark is poked, prodded, or molested. It may then protect itself by biting.

Leopard Shark *(Triakis semifasciata)*

The leopard shark belongs to the family of smooth dogfishes, a family of sharks (Triakidae) that inhabits shallow warm to tropical seas around the world. All of these sharks are small, usually three feet (90 cm) or less, but occasionally individuals grow to five feet (150 cm) long. The lower lobe of the tail is poorly developed. Many members of this family, which contains about thirty species, are harvested commercially as food.

They are widespread and can be pests in the nets of commercial fishermen. They have flat teeth for crushing shells.

All smooth dogfishes, including the leopard shark, are considered harmless. But it must be remembered that, with few exceptions, any animal is likely to bite in self-defense if it is bothered. These sharks are also easily excited by and attracted to even small traces of blood in the water. Leopard sharks, which occur off the Pacific coast of North America from Oregon southward to Baja California, have been known to attack divers without provocation. The most attractive of its family, the leopard shark's name comes from the splotches of black on a yellowish background.

Tiger Shark *(Galeocerdo cuvieri)*

Averaging more than ten feet (3 m) long but with 18-footers (5.5 m) not uncommon and unauthenticated reports of individuals 30 feet (9.1 m) long, this dangerous giant roams warm to tropical seas around the world. This is one of the requiem, or "typical," sharks, with its torpedo-shaped body, its first dorsal fin large and far forward, and the second dorsal small and located just above the anal fin. The upper lobe of its large tail is sickle-shaped. Young tiger sharks are striped with vertical **51**

▲ Leopard shark

black bars on a grayish background, but these marks become less distinct as the shark matures.

Though it generally stays in offshore waters, the blunt-nosed tiger shark may wander close to shore when prowling for food. It feeds on fish, turtles, rays, or any other animals in its path, even including other tiger sharks. Because many have been slaughtered—heavily harvested both for their oil and their hides—the contents of numerous stomachs have been examined, revealing an astonishing assortment of indigestibles, such as bottles, cans, automobile tires, chicken coops, deer antlers, and other items. They have also contained the gory, partly digested remains of a variety of animals, including humans. The tiger shark has a world-wide reputation as a man-eater, and there are records to substantiate that this is one of the most dangerous of all sharks. Unless feeding, however, the tiger shark is quite sluggish and does not attack just for the sport of it. The great variety of items taken from its stomach is at least partly explained by the shark's scavenging habits, for it soon learns to find its meals at man's dumping areas in the sea.

The tiger shark is viviparous and may bear as many as 50 young at a time, with reports of as many as 80. The young are about 1½ feet (45 cm) long at birth.

Blue Shark *(Prionace glauca)*

This slim, swift shark, averaging about ten feet (3 m) but known to be twice as long, is a pelagic species that roams warm seas around the world. One of the most handsome of all sharks, it is bright blue above and white below. Often it is seen basking with its dorsal and tail fins above the surface. It commonly follows ships to scavenge garbage. Sometimes, though not often, it comes close to shore in its search for food. Both sailors and fishermen fear this shark because it moves in so boldly to get its meals, but despite its long-standing reputation for being a rascal, there are no authenticated records of a blue shark **52** actually attacking a human. It is definitely on the suspect list,

▲ Tiger shark ▼ Blue shark

however, and should not be considered harmless. The potential is there: a voracious appetite, sharp teeth, and greed to get its share of whatever might be edible in the sea. Like the tiger shark, it gives birth to many young, sometimes more than 50.

Bull Shark *(Carcharinus leucas)*

One of the so-called ground sharks, a large genus that frequents rather shallow inshore and brackish waters, the bull shark also travels far up rivers. Where it has become landlocked in Lake Nicaragua, more than a hundred miles (160 km) from the sea, the bull shark is notorious for its attacks on humans. Although it is a sluggish swimmer, it can become quite savage when feeding. The bull shark is commonly seen scavenging under bridges or around piers. It grows to an average of six feet (1.8 m), but it may attain a length of ten feet (3 m) and weigh as much as 400 pounds (181 kg). This shark is often seen in inshore waters, and while it is normally only inquisitive when it swims this close, it should not be trusted and certainly not taunted. It is also known by such names as cub shark, fish shark, and ground shark.

Sandbar Shark *(Carcharinus milberti)*
Also called New York ground shark, this shark is found in
temperate to cool coastal waters of the Atlantic off both North
America and Europe. Like the bull shark, its counterpart in
habits and appearance in warm seas, the sandbar shark sometimes travels far up streams and appears regularly in brackish
waters. Its average length is about six feet (1.8 m), but individuals twice as long are now and then reported. This shark
does not have an authenticated record of having attacked
humans, but it is nevertheless listed as potentially dangerous. **55**
◄ Bull shark ▲ Sandbar shark

White-tipped Shark *(Pterolamiops longimanus)*

A relative of the bull and sandbar sharks, the white-tipped shark ranges around the world; it is most prevalent in subtropical and tropical seas but sometimes wanders into cooler waters. The tips of its dorsal fins are typically white, but can also be grayish. Its rather thick body may exceed 12 feet (3.6 m) in length. It has a short, heavy snout. The white-tipped shark is the most sea-going of the ground sharks, although it also appears from time to time in inshore waters. Like others in its group, it is feared, but there has been no record of its having attacked humans.

Dusky Shark *(Carcharinus obscurus)*

Another of the ground sharks, the dusky shark frequents the coasts of both Europe and North America and is also seen in the open sea. The dusky shark is not distinctive in color (a lead gray) or pattern and is easily confused with other ground sharks. A prominent ridge between its two dorsal fins is its most identifying feature. It may reach a length of 14 feet (4.3 m). Like its relatives, it should be regarded with caution but has never been known to harm humans.

Dusky shark▲ White-tipped shark ▶

Small Black-tipped Shark *(Carcharinus limbatus)*

A ground shark inhabiting the Atlantic, the small black-tipped shark, or spinner (so-called because it often ''spins'' its body when it leaps from the sea), is primarily pelagic, only rarely coming close to shore. Though it is a mainly subtropical or tropical species, it sometimes strays northward in summer and is often seen off the coast of Massachusetts. Its body is a dull gray, but the black tips on its fins are distinct and identifying. It averages six feet (1.8 m) in length. At times it will leap high out of the water and then somersault back into the sea. When hooked, it may perform these acrobatics or may become a dead weight and allow itself to be brought to gaff without a struggle. Again, this species is not considered highly dangerous, but if provoked it can do much harm.

Large Black-tipped Shark *(Carcharinus maculipinnis)*
Resembling the small black-tipped shark but larger (the two species not separated by all authorities), the large black-tipped shark has smaller eyes and longer gill slits. It occurs in the same waters and has similar habits. This species has a record of at least one unprovoked attack on a swimmer.

Bay Shark *(Carcharinus lamiella)*
Reaching a maximum length of 15 feet (4.6 m), the bay shark is another of the ground shark group. It ranges from southern California southward along the coast of Mexico. Its name comes from the fact that it is often observed in San Diego Bay. The bay shark is yellowish brown or bronze. It feeds both as a predator and scavenger in the relatively shallow coastal waters. Like its relatives, it is potentially dangerous, but there are **58** no verified reports of attacks on humans.

▲ Small black-tipped shark

Whalers (*Carcharinus macrurus, ahenea*, and others)
Several species of ground sharks living in Australian waters are known collectively as whalers, and they are ranked among the most dangerous sharks of the region because of their frequently reported attacks on humans. Their name is derived from their habit of swarming around harpooned whales to get their share of the kill—and sometimes most of it. Most of the whalers are about ten feet (3 m) long. The common species are the brown, bronze, black, and South Australian varieties.

Lemon Shark (*Negaprion brevirostris*)
The lemon shark is especially common in the Caribbean, but it also roams warm waters throughout the world. This inshore species is usually about six feet (1.8 m) long but may grow to ten feet (3 m). Its belly is distinctly yellow, accounting for its name. In some areas it is known as yellow shark. Its back and **59**

▲ Whaler shark

sides are yellowish brown. The lemon shark has a broad, rounded snout, and compared to other requiem sharks its first dorsal fin is smaller and the second proportionately larger—the two almost the same size. Though the lemon shark is ordinarily harmless, it does have an unpredictable disposition and has been known to attack humans. It should definitely be avoided.

Hammerhead Sharks *(Sphyrna* spp.)
These unusual sharks (there are more than half a dozen species) are distinguished from all others by their flattened heads with eyes and nostrils located at the tips of these hammerlike extensions. In the typical species, these extensions are blunt-ended; in those called bonnet sharks, the extensions are rounded or scalloped. The sharks use these mallets as rudders or planes against the water, giving them greater maneuverability than most sharks. They prowl the shallows of warm to tropical seas around the world and are fast swimmers, moving in quickly at the slightest trace of blood in the water. Like most sharks, they are not discriminating and will eat virtually anything that moves. Some seem to have an unusual penchant for

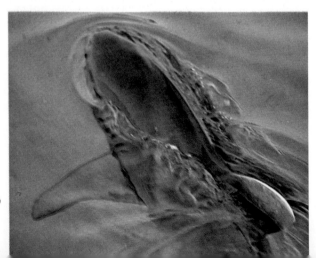

stingrays and appear also to be little affected by the spines, which are found lodged in their jaws and other parts of the their body.

The largest is the great hammerhead *(S. mokarran,)* which may reach a length of more than 15 feet (4.6 m) and weigh 1,500 pounds (680 kg). In a shark this size, the span of the ''hammers'' may exceed three feet (91 cm) across. The great hammerhead roams all warm seas and may even appear in brackish waters.

The bonnethead or bonnet shark *(S. tiburo)* has a rounded or kidney-shaped head, much like a shovel. Usually less than five feet (1.5 m) long, it occurs in the same waters as the great hammerhead and the other species with flattened head extensions.

The bonnethead is not considered at all dangerous to humans, but the hammerheads are distinctly so. They have small teeth but big mouths, and they will swallow whole (or at least make the attempt) almost anything that moves in the water or drops from a boat.

61

◀ Lemon shark ▲ Hammerhead shark

Other Fish That Bite

3

If your acquaintance with fish is limited to the toothless goldfish in a bowl and you have the notion that fish have only gums and fat lips, you have much to learn about fish of the sea. Any saltwater fisherman can tell you which fish can bite—most of them. Unless you positively know better, it is best to consider all marine fish as having a potentially bothersome to dangerous bite. With this approach, you will be sure of keeping all your fingers.

Many marine fish do have numerous sharp, daggerlike teeth, short in some species but long in others. Some have teeth fused into a pointed beak, razor-sharp and powerful enough to snip wires or fingers in two. Almost all have strong jaw muscles and can hold on tenaciously. Most kinds bite only in self-defense or as a reflex action when a finger or a hand is poked into their mouth to remove a hook. A few kinds, however, are actually aggressive and pugnacious, easily provoked into making attacks. But no matter why they bite, the pain is the same.

◀ Yellowfin grouper

Barracudas *(Sphyraena spp.)*

Most divers are more afraid of barracudas than of sharks. This is partly because barracudas themselves are so unafraid. Often they will follow a diver, swim in close for a look, and then move off again. Fortunately they rarely attack, but sometimes it happens. Triggered by some unexplainable impulse — perhaps flashing bright objects or quick, jerky movements—a barracuda may aim its torpedo-shaped body directly for a diver's arm or leg. A barracuda's bite is a clean-edged shear, the attack swift and forceful. Many barracudas are caught by sport fishermen, and they give an exciting battle before tiring. But even a tired barracuda still has sharp teeth! It can usually muster sufficient energy to close its jaws on probing fingers or hands that are trying to remove a hook or lure.

More than twenty species of barracudas roam the warm **64** waters of the world. One of the largest of these fish is the great

Great barracuda ▲

barracuda *(S. barracuda)*, which occurs off the coast of Florida and in the Caribbean. Though it averages only about three feet (90 cm) or less in length, individuals to eight feet (244 cm) long have been reported. Other species of barracudas are no more than a foot long. There are only a few barracuda species that have been directly credited with attacks on humans. The majority of the victims survive, but some have died from loss of blood or from shock, and some have lost an arm or leg, the amputation generally completed or nearly so by the barracuda. Attacks typically take place in shallow waters—even in knee-deep wading areas along beaches. Barracudas are bold enough to move into groups of bathers. Large barracudas are solitary hunters; smaller ones generally travel in packs. The savagery and bloodthirstiness of barracudas is greatly exaggerated, true, but these prowling predators are definitely dangerous and should be heeded with caution. **65**

Moray Eels *(Gymnothorax, Echidna, Mureana, etc.)*

Like barracudas, morays have a reputation for having nasty dispositions, and at times they seem to go out of their way to bite. But keep in mind that the morays only really bite intruders—people who blunder into their hideaways. No moray, barracuda, shark, or any other fish ever comes out on land to chase a man. The sea is their world.

There are more than 80 species of morays, and all of them live in subtropical and tropical seas but occasionally follow warm currents far out of their normal range. Many are handsome—green, yellow, maroon, rich brown, or black, with bright spots and stripes in contrasting colors. Some are less than a foot long, but five to six feet (1.5–1.8 m) is average, a few attaining a length of ten feet (3 m). All are eel-like or snakelike in body shape. Typically, they inhabit coral reefs, selecting a particular crevice or cranny as their lair. With two-thirds or more of its body anchored in the coral, the moray lets the front portion sway in the current, looking deceptively like some straplike growth of seaweed. But whatever comes close is fair game for the moray; it attacks either to get a meal or to protect its territory. Its mouth is gaped, and inside is a formidable array of teeth ready to sink into any unfortunate victim, large or small. The big knifelike teeth are curved backward like a snake's so that it is almost impossible for prey to **66** free itself from the moray's mouth once the jaws are shut.

Moray eel ▲

A moray's bite is not poisonous, but the bite wound is likely
to be jagged and torn due to the difficulty of detaching the big,
slippery eel after it has clamped its jaws shut. Bites should be
given medical attention immediately to stop the loss of blood
and also to prevent infection, which can be more dangerous
than the bite itself.

Groupers (*Epinephelus, Lates, Myeteroperca,* etc.)
Groupers belong to a family (Serranidae) of more than 400
species that are most commonly found in warm seas. Many are
caught by anglers. All groupers have sharp teeth and can bite,
though the small ones rarely do much harm. A bite from a big
grouper can be severe, however, and some of these giants are
actually large enough—500 to nearly 1,000 pounds (220–
4,540 kg)—to swallow a person whole. The big ones lurk in
"holes," or lairs, and move around only in the near vicinity to
find their meals. They are fearless, and some become aggressive when approached by divers, many of whom have reported "attacks" by these monsters. There are accounts, too, **67**

▲ Nassau grouper

▲ Parrotfish ▼ Bluefish

of divers in the South Pacific who have disappeared in waters where big groupers live, and some authorities speculate that they could only have become meals for these big fish.

Parrotfishes *(Scarus, Sparisema, Callyodon, etc.)*

As many as a hundred species of parrotfishes inhabit coral-reef waters around the world. Some are as much as ten feet (3 m) long; most are only a foot long. Many are brightly colored, some with rainbow combinations. But all share one feature—a thick, sharp parrotlike beak which they use to crush the limy skeletons of coral animals to get at the soft insides. This beak is not truly a weapon, but a parrotfish will instinctively clamp its mouth tightly, cutting in two anything that comes between its jaws. Playing with a parrotfish is a bit like playing Russian roulette if you value your fingers.

Bluefish *(Pomatomus saltatrix)*

Anyone who has seen a school of bluefish chop its way through a shoal of menhaden, herring, or other fish needs no advice about keeping his or her hands away from this voracious creature's mouth. In the sea, bluefish have no parallels. They are the marine complements of the dreaded piranhas of South American freshwater streams. The average weight of a bluefish is about three pounds (1.3 kg), though a record catch on rod and reel weighed 31 pounds 8 ounces (14 kg). It was taken off Cape Hatteras, North Carolina. Bluefish are found in the Atlantic off the coasts of North and South America, the schools moving north in summer and then returning south again in winter. Bluefish are popular with sport fishermen because they will take almost any bait or lure offered and then put up a game fight when hooked. They are also taken in nets by commercial fishermen because they are considered one of the tastiest of the fish caught along these coasts. But wise anglers handle them with great care at all times. **69**

Sea Snakes

4

All of the sea-dwelling snakes—about fifty species—are poisonous, and all live in the warm waters of the South Pacific, off the coasts of Australia and southern Asia, and near many of the islands. One species, the yellow-bellied sea snake, sometimes appears off the western coasts of South and Central America. No sea snakes, at present, are found in Atlantic or Caribbean waters, though an invasion by way of the Panama Canal is possible. Sea snakes are usually most abundant in shallow coastal waters, and some species also wander into freshwater streams. A few species venture ashore to lay their eggs, but most kinds give birth to their young at sea.

A sea snake's body is greatly flattened from side to side and the tail even more so, an adaptation to their aquatic life. Most sea snakes have scales that fit one against the other like bricks in a wall rather than overlapping. They must come to the surface for air, although they are believed to be able to remain submerged for an hour or longer. Typically their nostrils open on top of the snout, permitting the snakes to breathe while swimming or basking at the surface. No one knows how deep they can dive, but they have been observed feeding at depths of thirty feet (9.1 m). Most of them have the curious habit of diving straight down rather than on a slanted course, as most sea ani-

◄ Annulated sea snake

mals do. Almost all sea snakes are helpless on land. They lack the broad, flat ventral scales that give land-dwelling snakes traction on ground surfaces.

Sea snakes use their venom in killing prey. They make their meals of fish, though some kinds will also eat shrimp or other animals. They are docile but deadly—at least some of them. Most of them try to escape if caught in nets and ordinarily make no attempt to bite. The bites usually occur when a snake is accidentally stepped on in shallow water or when a fisherman is trying to get a snake out of a net. Sea snakes have small fangs, and some must chew to inject their venom, leaving a wound with multiple punctures. The venom is a neurotoxin, and the poison of some species is said to be more potent than a king cobra's. Like many other neurotoxins, it may have a delayed effect. A person bitten by a sea snake should be kept in a hospital or under close medical attention for a day or longer even if he appears to be all right. A collapse of the respiratory mechanism due to paralysis can come quickly.

During the breeding season, thousands of sea snakes may collect in a particular area in the sea and mill at the surface. Sea snakes are at this time most aggressive and should be avoided.

In the Orient, some kinds of sea snakes are harvested as food—prized as a delicacy, in fact. The hides of some are tanned for leather.

Yellow Sea Snake *(Hydrophis spiralis)*
Believed to be the longest of the sea snakes—averaging about five feet (1.5 m) but known to exceed nine (2.1 m)—this colorful snake is a bright golden yellow, sometimes with a greenish tinge. Its belly is white. Black rings circle the body from head to tail. The yellow sea snake is generally found in relatively deep water, but it also comes to the surface to bask. Though its venom is not the most potent, several deaths resulting from its bite are recorded.

▲Sea snakes from Great Barrier Reef in Australia▼

Pelagic or Yellow-bellied Sea Snake *(Pelamis platurus)*
The pelagic sea snake is the only species that regularly inhabits the open sea, where it seems to spend much of its time floating at the surface. It does regularly appear near shores, however, and large numbers of this species have been observed off the western coasts of tropical South and Central America. Unlike other sea snakes, it apparently never enters fresh or brackish waters, and in fact it appears to make a special effort to avoid them.

The pelagic sea snake averages about two feet (61 cm) in length, and reaches a maximum of four feet (120 cm). Its body is eel-like, the tail strongly compressed. Perhaps the most

Yellow-bellied sea snake ▲

striking of all the sea snakes, most are dark brown or black above and bright yellow below. There are several other color varieties. In one the tail is barred or mottled with black. This snake's venom is one of the lowest in toxicity, and only one human death has been recorded, the identification of the snake questionable.

Hardwicke's Sea Snake *(Lapemis hardwickii)*
One of the thick-bodied sea snakes, Hardwicke's averages two feet (61 cm) in length, rarely three feet (90 cm). It is yellowish green with broad dark bands that become distinct bars on its tail. The broad head is wider than the neck. This

snake is common off the Philippines and southeastern Asia, where it is frequently caught in nets, particularly during the summer months. Several deaths have been attributed to its bite.

Beaked Sea Snake *(Emyhydrinas schistosa)*

The beaked sea snake inhabits the shallow waters of bays, estuaries, and rivers off southeastern Asia. Its lower jaw is distinctive because of the smallness of the chin scale, or shield, which allows the snake to open its mouth extraordinarily wide in order to swallow large prey. The scale covering the top of its snout turns down, forming a "beaked" profile. Over much of its body, and most particularly in the neck region, the skin is exceptionally loose. Averaging three feet (90 cm) long, the beaked sea snake is gray to greenish above and whitish below with distinct dark bands on the middle and rear which

76 tend to fuse toward the front of the body. The head is dark, the

▲ Beaked sea snake ▲ Annulated sea snake

tail mottled. The young are all white with black bands, their colors becoming brighter as they mature.

The beaked sea snake has one of the most potent venoms of all poisonous snakes both on land or in the sea, and a number of deaths are attributed to its bite. The snake is abundant along heavily populated coasts, but it is not aggressive.

Annulated Sea Snake (Hydrophis cyanocinctus)

Common in mangrove swamps but also seen ten miles (16 km) or more at sea, the annulated sea snake is white to greenish with black crossbands, some of which do not completely encircle the body. This snake averages more than four feet (1.2 m) in length, some individuals attaining a length of six feet (1.8 m). Though its venom is not the most potent, the annulated sea snake causes a number of deaths annually because of its abundance near centers of population off the coast of south-eastern Asia.

Shockers 5

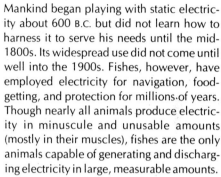

Mankind began playing with static electricity about 600 B.C. but did not learn how to harness it to serve his needs until the mid-1800s. Its widespread use did not come until well into the 1900s. Fishes, however, have employed electricity for navigation, food-getting, and protection for millions of years. Though nearly all animals produce electricity in minuscule and unusable amounts (mostly in their muscles), fishes are the only animals capable of generating and discharging electricity in large, measurable amounts.

The ancient Egyptians, Greeks, and Romans knew that some fishes could produce powerful shocks, but they did not understand how or why. The Greeks called the electric ray *narke,* from which our word narcotic is derived. Some of the physicians of the day recommended the use of shocks in treating nervous disorders, similar to the methods prescribed in recent times. But they also suggested other uses that were based on the supposed mystical powers of these rays, or numbfish. Each discovery of a new kind of electric fish caused a flurry of new speculations about how the shocks were produced.

In addition to marine electric or torpedo rays, of which there are about 30 species throughout the world, there are roughly 20 species of electric stargazers, which occur in abundance in warm waters. Electricity is also produced by mormyrids, or Nilepikes (also called "elephant fishes" because of their trunklike snouts), and by electric cat- **79**

◄ California electric ray

fish, both of which live in freshwaters of tropical Africa. Of all electric fishes, however, the freshwater South American electric eel is the most dangerous and most powerful. Capable of discharging 600 volts in pulsing jolts of 400 per second for extended periods, it is powerful enough to kill a person ten feet (3 m) away. An electric eel grows quite large, weighing as much as 90 pounds (41 kg), with about fifty percent of its weight accounted for by its electric organs.

Some torpedo or electric rays can produce shocks of 200 volts, the stargazers about 50 volts maximum. Though these marine fish are not as powerful as the freshwater electric eel and their discharges are dissipated quickly by saltwater, they are nevertheless strong enough to be annoying or even dangerous. Their electric organs evolved from muscles but are now highly specialized. They consist of disclike, multinucleate cells, or electroplates, arranged one against the other in columns that are set in a jellylike matrix and surrounded by connective tissues. Each column is supplied with nerves and blood vessels. The electricity generated by each cell is added to the next, producing a cumulative voltage total. In a large electric ray, a million or more cells may be generating electricity in these organic batteries. The cells are arranged so that a ray is positive on its top surface, negative below. (In freshwater electric catfish and also electric eels, the polarity is the opposite: that is, negative above and positive below.)

In aquarium exhibits, the electricity produced by electric rays is used to ring bells or to light bulbs to demonstrate that a current is actually there. The ray controls the emissions by its nerves, which connect the electric organs directly to the brain. The organs themselves are clearly visible as round structures in each "wing" or pectoral fin near the head.

Almost as amazing as the ability of these fishes to generate electricity is their immunity to the shock themselves—either their own or that produced by the fishes around them. This has **80** not been thoroughly researched or explained, but with the

development of the electric organs in the fish, an effective insulator has evolved, composed mainly of thick layers of fat.

All of the electric rays are sluggish and ordinarily lie on the bottom partly covered with sand or mud, some close to shore and others in deep water. It is, of course, the shallow-water species that are most commonly encountered. They are poor swimmers, and compared to the more speedy true rays, they have a soft, almost spongy flattened body. They feed on a variety of worms, crustaceans, and other animals found on the bottom and do not in normal circumstances need to use their electricity. But if an animal attempts to escape, the electric ray can give it a stunning, debilitating shock. Similarly, the electric ray may use its shocks for protection if in danger, though it has virtually no natural enemies. One encounter is sufficiently discouraging to prevent a predator from making a second try. Some investigators suggest that the rays may also give off short pulses of electricity that echo back from objects, providing a radarlike navigational mechanism. If this is true, it is effective only for short distances but would still be useful in muddy water where there is low visibility. Researchers also suggest that electrical pulses of this sort might be used in identification of species or possibly even of sexes.

Electric rays are worldwide in distribution but are only locally abundant at times in some areas. Any fisherman, diver, or swimmer is likely to encounter an electric ray, and should **81**

▲ Eagle ray

be alert to this possibility. A shock may be painful or powerful enough to knock someone over, depending both on the size of the ray and on the person's condition. Fortunately the rays do discharge themselves quickly—after only a dozen or so jolts. No deaths or serious injuries have been recorded.

Atlantic Torpedo *(Torpedo nobilana)*

The largest of the electric rays, the Atlantic torpedo may measure to six feet (1.8 m) long and weigh as much and 200 pounds (91 kg), although the average is 30 pounds (14 kg). It occurs on both sides of the Atlantic and also in the Mediterranean. Torpedo, also the generic name for this ray, is derived from the Latin word *torpid,* meaning slow or inactive. All of the species in this genus have blunt, almost truncated noses, and their close-set eyes are on top of their head, just behind the nose. The central body is dark with no markings and is nearly round. Jolts of 220 volts have been recorded.

California Electric Ray *(Torpedo californica)*

The California electric ray is similar in appearance and habits to the Atlantic torpedo but is not quite as large. Fifty pounds (23 kg) is the maximum weight, and most are much smaller. It occurs on the Pacific coast from British Colombia southward to Mexican waters, occurring most abundantly off southern California.

Lesser Electric Ray *(Narcine brasiliensis)*

This small electric ray is found in warm Atlantic waters from North Carolina southward to Brazil. Though it may reach a length of 1½ feet (46 cm), it is usually less than a foot long. Its snout is pointed, and its yellowish-tan body is blotched with black spots rather than solid dark as in the Atlantic torpedo. Other electric rays include the Australian numbfish *(Narcine tasmaniensis),* rarely more than a foot long, hence not very powerful; the Australian crampfish *(Hypnarce monopterygium),* with a blobby, tail-less body; the New Zealand blind torpedo *(Typhlonarke aysoni),* which lacks functional eyes and uses its ventral fins like legs; and the South American electric ray *(Diplobatus pictus),* which has a more elongate, almost sharklike body than do the typical electric rays.

83

◀ Atlantic torpedo ▲ Lesser electric ray

Electric Stargazers *(Astroscopus)*

The electric organs of these stargazers are located just behind the eyes and have apparently evolved from tissues of the optic nerves rather than from muscles. Discharges up to 50 volts have been recorded, but they are usually less. To a human, this is a distinct and disturbing jolt but is not dangerous.

Stargazers are fat-bodied, ugly, sand- or mud-colored fish that lie buried in the bottom of the sea with only their eyes above the surface. Their eyes are on top of their head and are directed upward—"gazing at the stars," so to speak. Unique among fish, some stargazers breathe through their nostrils, which connect to their throat and gill cavity rather than being blind pouches as in most fishes. This solves the problem they would have of taking in mud or sand if they breathed through their mouth when buried. Some species have a wormlike

structure inside their mouth which is displayed enticingly when the mouth is opened. If a potential meal, such as a shrimp or a small fish, comes close enough to investigate the lure, the stargazer stuns it with a jolt of electricity and then comes out of hiding to swallow its catch. The electricity may also be used to discourage and scare away intruders or predators, though stargazers have few natural enemies.

Stargazers have sharp, grooved spines above each pectoral fin. These connect to venom glands that produce a toxin potent enough to kill a person (see p. 123).

The approximately two dozen species of electric stargazers are widely distributed in temperate to warm and shallow to deep seas throughout the world.

Northern Stargazer *(Astroscopus guttatus)*
To as much as 1½ feet (46 cm) long but usually much less, the northern stargazer is found in shallow waters from Cape Hatteras northward to New York.

Southern Stargazer *Astroscopus y-graecum)*
About a third smaller than the northern stargazer, this species ranges southward from Cape Hatteras through the West Indies to Brazil.

European Stargazer *(Uranoscopus scaber)*
About 12 inches (30 cm) long at maximum and generally smaller, the European stargazer inhabits temperate to warm coastal waters off Europe.

◀ Southern stargazer ▲ Australian crampfish

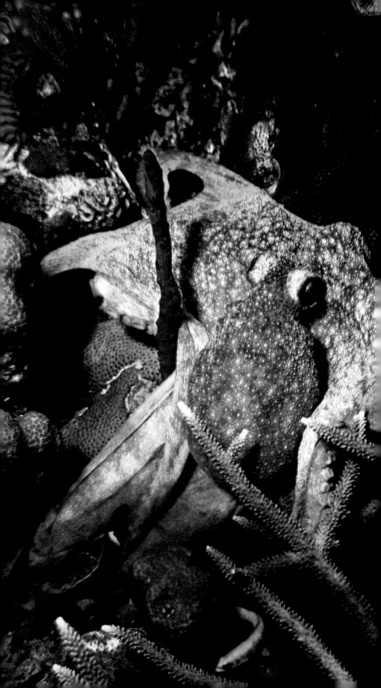

Stinging Animals

Of all the animals in the sea, those that sting are the most dangerous to human beings. Some are only bothersome, their stings merely a nettling sensation that is over quickly, but included in this group, too, are the most deadly sea creatures, capable of killing swiftly and subtly. Believe it or not, in the strange world of the sea, jellies are more dangerous than jaws, popular notions to the contrary. The most deadly of the animals are those without backbones, or invertebrates. Most do not appear able to deliver a death-dealing punch. With the exception of the octopuses that have a venomous bite, the poisons of these animals are injected by spines or dart mechanisms. They are used by the animals primarily in self-defense and to a lesser degree to kill or stun prey. None attack humans in the manner that sharks or barracudas do.

The venoms are commonly described as being either neurotoxic or hemotoxic, but most of these venoms have both effects. Neurotoxins are "nerve" poisons that spread rapidly and cause death by paralysis of respiratory mechanisms. Hemotoxins are less rapid and are most effective locally, breaking down tissues in the immediate vicinity of the sting. To say that one is worse than the other is not of great usefulness, however, for a purely neurotoxic or hemotoxic venom is rare. Further, in sufficient amounts and potency, both can kill.

87

◀ Octopus

Good from the Deadly

A brief credit note is due these deadly creatures of the sea. Poisons from any animals are nature's most powerful chemicals, and since earliest times mankind has used them in various ways to combat illnesses, literally "fighting fire with fire." The theory is simple: if a poison is strong enough to kill, then it can also kill the tiny microscopic organisms that cause infection. This is a gross oversimplification, of course, but it is the essential truth that guides the use of drugs in medicine. In modern medical research, venoms are broken down chemically into their basic components (all are highly complex amino acids or proteins), and then each of the specific elements is tested for its potential use in treating a variety of ailments—from nervous disorders and ulcers to heart diseases and cancer. Since they are natural compounds, venoms are more acceptable to a person's vital parts. Though they are many times more powerful per unit than synthetic compounds, they are less damaging.

The details of research being done are fascinating, but here it suffices to say that the venomous creatures of the sea may benefit mankind, doing much more good than harm. Killers of the sea are in this way being converted into valued curers of some of mankind's plaguing physical and emotional ills.

In the following descriptions, the groups of animals are discussed from the most primitive, the coelenterates, to the most advanced, the bony fishes.

Coelenterates

Among the broad groups of animals (the phyla), only the one-celled animals, or protozoans, and the sponges are lower in the scale of life than are coelenterates. All of the some 10,000 species are marine creatures, with the exception of familiar freshwater hydras. Included in the group are jellyfishes, sea anemones, corals, and saltwater relatives of hydras. All of the coelenterates share certain basic features. Each

body is organized in a circle around a central axis: that is, it has radial symmetry rather than bilateral (duplicated right and left halves) as in fish, shrimp, and other higher animals. The body consists of an outer layer of cells (ectoderm) and an inner layer (endoderm) with a jellylike substance between them. This middle layer generally contains no cells, but some species have drifting cells that perform special functions.

Internally there is a single cavity, or coelom, which has only one opening to the exterior. This serves as a mouth for taking in food and is also the opening through which indigestible wastes are cast out of the body. The mouth is surrounded by tentacles that help some species with locomotion but are basically used in obtaining food and then passing it to the mouth. Concentrated in the tentacles but sometimes scattered over the body are microscopic stinging capsules, or nematocysts, used by the animals in stunning or killing their prey. They are also powerful weapons and can be fatal to humans. **89**

▲ Sea anemone

A typical nematocyst consists of a pear-shaped cell containing a coiled, threadlike filament that ends in a sharp barb. The nematocyst is covered by a lid, or operculum, and somewhere near this lid on the outer surface is a triggering mechanism, or cnidocil. When the cnidocil is touched or in some cases when stimulated by a chemical change in the water, the lid pops off the nematocyst and the contents of the cell are everted explosively. The filament becomes a tiny harpoonlike missile that is driven forcefully into any object in its path. It may, for example, penetrate even a glove and still have force enough to go through the skin of a finger. At the same time, the cell contracts and forces the venom inside to be squirted down the hollow filament and out its tip into the wound.

Some coelenterates have several types of nematocysts—kinds with barbs and others that are barbless; kinds that lack venom but are long and slim, coiling or looping around whatever they touch; kinds that are sticky so that they adhere to an object rather than penetrating it; and kinds that are designed especially for injecting venom. A single nematocyst is so minute that it cannot contain enough venom to be harmful to a human, but one tentacle of some of the larger animals may have 100,000 or more nematocysts. In animals with dozens of tentacles, the potential amount of poison from the discharge of all of the nematocysts becomes great. There is no central controlling mechanism for the firing of the nematocysts, however. Each operates individually, and once a nematocyst is discharged, it cannot be retracted. It is cast out, and a new one develops to take its place.

Portuguese Man-o-war (Physalia physalis)

The Portuguese man-o-war is a member of the same group of coelenterates as the freshwater hydras. One Portuguese man-o-war is actually made up of a colony of individuals that perform different functions aiding in the survival of the group. **90** Some cells, for example, are strictly food-getters; others digest

the animals passed to them by the tentacles. The function of others is reproduction, and still others maintain the gas-filled float by which the Portuguese man-o-war sails the seas.

The Portuguese man-o-war is indeed one of the spectacles of seas around the world. Its sausage-shaped bubble, with a crinkly or scalloped crest, rides above the surface of the sea so that the colony is swept along by the currents or is blown by the winds. When the winds blow toward shore, the Portuguese man-o-war may appear in the shallows of beach areas or be cast onto the shore in countless numbers. At these times the beaches post warnings and are closed to bathers, for this unusual, attractive creature is one of the most dangerous of all sea animals.

Off the Atlantic coast of North America, for example, the Portuguese man-o-war may begin to appear along the beaches **91**

▲ Sea anemone at night

in October. At this time the floats are still small—no bigger than eggs. But as the months go by, the colonies grow larger, and by early spring, some are as much as a foot (30 cm) long and stand six inches (15 cm) or more above the surface. By late spring or early summer they have disappeared, making the beaches safe again for a few months.

But it is the full-grown ones that are most dangerous. Around the rim of their float are dozens of tentacles that sometimes contract to stubby fingerlike structures but generally trail out into the sea as streamers, which can be 50 feet (15.2 m) long but are usually 10–20 feet (3–6 m). The function of these tentacles is to find and kill food (tiny crustaceans, small fish, and similar creatures). A Portuguese man-o-war may be armed with half a million or more nematocysts, each **92** containing minute amounts of venom that is chemically akin

▲ Portuguese man-o-war with tentacles knotted beneath the float

to the toxin of cobras and only about twenty-five percent less potent. The nematocysts are concentrated in "heads" along the tentacles so that when a person contacts a tentacle he may be impaled by literally hundreds of thousands of nematocysts.

The immediate effect is a shocking pain, an intense burning sensation that seems to radiate in all directions. If the stings are numerous, the victim experiences stomach cramps and dizziness, his muscles becoming taut and his breathing difficult. Heavy doses—fortunately rare—are followed by shock, paralysis, and death. Fatalities due to the Portuguese man-o-war have been recorded in Florida, the Virgin Islands, Texas, and the Pacific, and marine biologists believe that a fairly high percentage of deaths listed as accidental drownings or heart failure are due to the stings of these creatures. Unlike sharks, barracudas, and other animals that bite, the Portuguese man-o-war leaves no evidence of attack on its victim. The venom paralyzes the respiratory mechanism, so a person stung severely might logically be listed as a drowning victim with the real cause not recognized. The stings also cause shock, for the pain is immediate: pulsing, intense, and searing. When wrapped around the body the wispy, threadlike tentacles are nearly invisible but virtually impossible to scrape away, each delivering stabbing pains.

The Portuguese man-o-war is, in its way, a beautiful creature, its float an iridescent bluish purple and the crest tinged with orange-red. Though the float itself does not contain nematocysts, the tentacles can be deadly, their studding of stinging cells as lethal as the most venomous of all snakes on land or in the sea. Nor is the danger restricted to enounters in the water. When winds and waves wash these animals ashore, their tentacles become strewn over the sand. People walking barefoot on the beach, picking up shells or other objects, may suddenly feel a burning pain if they touch even a portion of a tentacle. In most cases of this sort, people receive only a few stings without much discomfort or long-lasting pain. **93**

In the sea, the chances of a person receiving a larger dosage are much greater. A Portuguese man-o-war's tentacles can trail far from the bubble that identifies the creature at the surface, and most people find themselves wrapped in a tentacle without ever suspecting that a Portuguese man-o-war is near. The multiple stings are not limited to arms or legs but may be on the neck, face, or chest—much nearer to vital organs. The pain is excruciating.

What can you do if you encounter one of these creatures? Get rid of tentacles and poison sacs as quickly as possible. The nematocysts themselves are too small to see, but you can see or feel the clinging tentacles. Scrub your skin with soap if you are near a shower, or use sand on the beach to help wad up and scrape off the tentacles. Ammonia, rubbing alcohol, or mineral oil will help relieve some of the pain, or some people sprinkle the stung area with meat tenderizer to "digest" the stings. If you are in the subtropics, the latex from the fruit or leaves of a papaya (the source of meat tenderizer) is a good natural source of digestive enzyme. If your stings are many or extensive, by all means see a doctor immediately.

Other animals of the sea are not immune to the venom of the Portuguese man-o-war, but some are remarkably daring. The little man-o-war fish, for example, lives in the drapery of the swaying tentacles, surviving by being alert and dodging. It darts out to get its meals of little crustaceans or other small animals but then quickly retreats inside the protective curtain to keep from being caught and eaten itself. It was once believed that this little fish was not affected by the poison, but research has shown that it, too, can be killed by the stings, though it can endure more venom than most animals can. Big sea turtles also have a remarkable ability to survive large doses of the poison. What pleasure they get from eating a Portuguese man-o-war or other jellyfish is not known, but they obviously relish them enough to endure swollen eyes and other evidences of the stings.

Fire Corals *(Millepona alicornis)*

Like the Portuguese man-o-war, the fire corals are marine relatives of freshwater hydras. They are not members of the true coral group. Fire corals grow in brownish mosslike masses on shells, pilings, true corals, and other objects, and they feed on microscopic creatures that swarm in the sea. Each tiny animal bears a tuft of tentacles surrounding its mouth, and when a mat of these animals is touched, the nematocysts in the tentacles are discharged. The pain is immediate—a hot burning sensation and a numbness or semiparalysis of the fingers or hand. Fortunately it does not last long. Avoid handling or touching objects in the sea with ungloved hands unless you know what they are.

▲ Fire coral

Sea Wasps (*Carydea* and *Chiropsalmus*)

Sea wasps are the most dangerous animals in the sea. True jellyfish, they belong to a group known more specifically as box jellies because their "bells" are flattened on four sides and nearly square. Their long tentacles hang down from tablike flaps at each of the four corners. Some kinds have only a single tentacle at each corner; others have groups of tentacles. Some of the box jellies are small, measuring only an inch or two across their bell; others are larger. All are found in shallow coastal waters from southern Japan southward through the Philippines to Australia.

The sea wasp, nearly the size of a person's head, has tentacles that may measure as much as 20 feet (6 m) long. It swims gracefully by pumping its bell. When it invades the shallow waters of beach areas it is almost impossible to see because of its transparency and is difficult to avoid. Children playing in knee-deep water have been victims of this jellyfish. The jellyfish does not "attack" in the literal sense of the word. When contacted, it reacts by discharging its nematocysts.

The venom is a powerful neurotoxin that takes effect with extraordinary speed. People stung by sea wasps may be dead **96** within five minutes after their encounter. Statistics on the

▲ Fire coral

actual number of fatalities caused by sea wasps are not available since the venom is effective so rapidly and no evidence of the stings is obvious. It is speculated that many reports of deaths due to drowning, heart failure, or similar causes might actually be due to sea wasps. One doctor in Brisbane, Australia, kept records of local deaths definitely attributed to sharks and to sea wasps for 25 years. His tally shows 13 deaths due to sharks and 60 due to sea wasps.

Other Jellyfish
The tentacles of many other jellyfish also bear stinging nematocysts, but the venom of most causes only temporary discomfort. At times of the year when beaches swarm with jellyfish, generally in late summer, people avoid going into the water. At this time, too, fishermen pull in nets filled with blobby masses of jellyfish but few fish. One common jellyfish found in the cool Atlantic waters off the coasts of North America and Europe and also ranging into the Pacific and Indian oceans is the sea nettle, its stings leaving a burning irritation that may persist for several days. The sea nettle measures only a few inches across its bell. Another animal that may be dangerous because of its size and the number of nematocysts that it can release is the giant pink jellyfish, known also as lion's mane jellyfish or sea blubber. Found in the cold waters of the northern Pacific and Atlantic, this big jellyfish may measure eight feet (2.4 m) across its bell, and its tentacles may stretch a hundred feet (30.5 m).

Corals *(Alcyonium, Acropora, Meancha, etc.)*
Coral reefs—among the most exciting places for divers—occur in warm waters in a belt around the world. The living coral animals are never in water more than 150 feet (45.7 m) deep or colder than 68° F (20° C). But the reef itself may be much deeper. It consists mainly of the limy skeletons of dead corals and other animals, the living organisms only forming **97**

the very top and side layers and living inside the stone cups of the dead corals. Some of the larger reefs have been in the process of building for at least 10,000 years.

Some of the islands forming the Florida Keys are the remains of old reefs. A living reef protected in an underwater park exists just off Key Largo. Great Barrier Reef along the eastern coast of Australia is the world's largest, extending for some 1,200 miles (1,920 km) and more than a hundred miles (160 km) wide in places. Many islands in the South Pacific consist entirely of coral. Atolls are coral islands that form a ring, sometimes broken in several places, around a central lagoon. **98** They are believed to be the remnants of reefs that once fringed

▲ Gorgonid, or horny, coral growing on base of stony coral

a mountaintop. As the sea gradually rose, the island was submerged, but the fringing reef around it continued to grow.

The many species of corals occur in a fantastic range of sizes, shapes, and colors. During the day the coral animals stay hidden in their stony cups, but at night they stretch out their tentacles to catch small animals on which they feed. Then the coral becomes a wriggling mass. Many other animals that live in the reef also become active at night.

Most corals can be touched without danger, but some kinds have powerful nematocysts that can penetrate the skin. Their venom is potent enough to be noticeable to a human. It is not only painful but may also cause a rash. More dangerous than **99**

▲ Sea anemone ▼ Powderpuff anemone

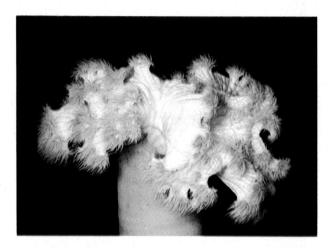

the stings, however, are the cuts, which after the initial pain heal slowly. This is commonly referred to as "coral poisoning." Why these coral cuts take so long to heal is not understood. Some authorities believe that a toxin enters the cut wound; others say it is simply due to a secondary infection. To avoid these annoying wounds, it is wise to wear heavy gloves when working with coral.

Sea Anemones *(Actinia, Sagartia, Adamsia, Anemonia,* etc.)
These "flowers of the sea" belong to the same group of coelenterates as corals, but their body is protected by a tough, leathery skin rather than a hard skeleton. Sea anemones spend most of their time fastened to shells, rocks, or other objects on the bottom, but they can also glide from place to place on their foot. Anemones feed by spreading the tentacles surrounding their mouth and waving them to attract and then catch small animals passing by in the water. At rest, they draw in their tentacles and shut their mouth. Most sea anemones are only three or four inches (8–10 cm) tall, but a giant that lives in Great Barrier Reef waters of Australia measures more than a foot (30 cm) tall and is about twice as broad across its base.

Like most coelenterates, sea anemones have stinging cells, or nematocysts, in their tentacles, and some kinds are more **101**
▲ Sea anemone

potent than others. The so-called "sponge fisherman's disease" is a rash of slow-healing welts that is produced by the stings of sea anemones. Sponge fishermen are regularly affected because they must cut their sponges from among the clusters of stinging sea anemones. Some of the sea anemones of the Indo-Pacific deliver punch enough in their stings to be rated potentially very dangerous, though none have been deadly to humans. The sedentary anemones depend on their poison to kill their meals and to provide them with protection. Like the Portuguese man-o-war and some of the true jellyfishes, however, sea anemones have become sanctuaries for some kinds of little fish that hide in the anemones' body cavity behind the shrubbery of poisonous tentacles. Presumably the little fishes are not greatly affected by the stings themselves, but they depend mainly on their agility to avoid being stung, benefitting by having a protective hideway into which they can escape after short food-hunting forays outside.

Mollusks

Mollusks are soft-bodied animals, some of which are protected by shells. They include oysters, clams, and other bivalves; snails (gastropods); chitons; and octopuses, squids, and nautili (cephalopods). In total there are more than 80,000 species, the greater percentage living in the sea. Some are dangerous to eat or may inflict some type of physical injury, but only the cone shells and some of the octopuses produce venom.

Cone Shells (Conus)

About 500 species of cone shells are recognized, nearly all of them inhabiting warm waters in the Indo-Pacific region. One species occurs off the coast of California, and a dozen or so are found in Gulf and Atlantic waters off southern United States. Almost all are attractive and colorful, making them highly prized by shell collectors. But the animal inside produces a

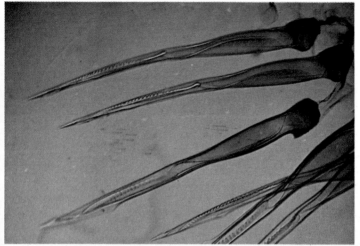
▲ Harpoonlike teeth of a cone shell ▼ Admiral cone, a venomous textile shell

venom and has an efficient means of injecting it. Though only a few species in the Indo-Pacific are rated as deadly, all living cone shells should be handled with extreme care.

The neurotoxic venom of cone shells is contained in a bulbous sac located behind their mouth opening, which is connected by a tube to the pharynx. The cone shell's tongue, or radula, bears a harpoonlike tooth at its tip, and when the tongue is forcefully protruded, it easily penetrates the skin. The poison sac is then contracted, and the venom flows directly into the wound. The stings are an effective means of defense and are used also by the carnivorous cone shells to kill or immobilize their prey, mainly other mollusks.

No one has analyzed the venoms of all cone shells to determine which are the most poisonous or potentially the most deadly, but all cone shells should be approached with caution. A number of deaths have been recorded, some occurring within only a few hours after the sting. The stinging is usually done so rapidly and deftly that the victim scarcely knows it has happened. At first he feels only a pain comparable to a bee sting, but soon there is a general numbness over most of his body. In fatal cases, death is attributed to heart failure caused by the poison.

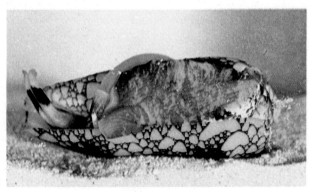

▲ Episcopal cone, a venomous textile cone shell

Octopuses *(Octopus)*

All octopuses have eight arms and bulbous bodies, and squids have eight arms plus two armlike tentacles and elongate bodies. Both are cephalopod mollusks that lack shells. (Other cephalopods are the cuttlefish, which have an internal shell, and nautili, which have compartmented shells.) Included in this group is the largest of all animals without backbones, the giant squid, known to reach a length of 60 feet (18.3 m). In contrast, some of the small octopuses measure only about two inches (5 cm) across their spread arms. Most octopuses and squids live in shallow water, occupying lairs in rocks or digging holes in soft bottoms. Some octopuses and squids are found in the deep sea, however they may come up from the depths to feed at night and then go back to the darkness of the deep water at night. Some species of octopuses secrete a venom to kill their prey that can be dangerous to humans. A few of the squids and cuttlefish have a venom, too, but it is very mild.

An octopus' mouth is a sharp, parrotlike beak. Prey is first caught in the arms, and with vigorous animals, sometimes all **105**

▲ *Octopus rubescens*

▲ Octopus

eight arms must be used in overcoming it. Along the arms are powerful suction cups that help in holding it. The prey is moved to the mouth where it is bitten and finally swallowed. At this time, too, some octopuses secrete a venom to subdue or kill a struggling catch. Precisely how this poison is passed to the victim is not clearly understood, but when the venom is released—from specialized salivary glands—it flows from the mouth into the bite wound or may even be absorbed by the gills of a fish or a crustacean without the need of a bite. The poison is a neurotoxin and works very rapidly in killing smaller animals, such as crabs. Death may occur in a minute or less.

The effect of octopus venom on humans depends on the size of the octopus and hence the amount of venom it can release. Also, the condition of the person being bitten is a factor, since some people are more sensitive or allergic than others. In cases where the octopuses have been small, measuring only 1–12 inches (2–30 cm) across their arms, the bites have been described as resembling severe bee stings. However, the pain and swelling may last for weeks or even months with the wound healing very slowly. There is only one authenticated record of a human death resulting from an encounter with an octopus, an animal that had an arm span of only about six inches (15 cm). This occurred in Australia. Other deaths have been reported but never confirmed. **107**

▲ Octopus

Annelids

Annelids are segmented worms, a group that includes leeches (mostly living in freshwater), earthworms (which burrow in moist soils), and marine worms (polychaetes). Some marine worms live near the shore, others occur at depths of three miles (4.8 km) or more. Some are free swimmers, using their paddlelike appendages to propel themselves through the water; others live in tubes in the sand or mud and extend only their plumelike gills, which are usually brightly colored and flowerlike. Respiration—the exchange of carbon dioxide for oxygen—occurs through the feathery plumes, which also trap plankton and pass it to the mouth.

Some marine worms produce a mild venom in glands at the base of the bristles, or setae, that occur in pairs on each of the body segments. These animals, called bristleworms, can sting. The bloodworms, another type, have strong jaws with which they can puncture skin and at the same time inject a venom. Neither animal is really dangerous. The effect of the venom is much like a normal bee sting and lasts for only a day or two, **108** sometimes producing a rash.

▲ Silky bristleworm on stony coral

Echinoderms

Echinoderms are the "spiny-skinned" animals of the sea, so named because almost all have spines on hard plates that are imbedded in their skin. Of the more than 5,000 species in this group, which includes the familiar starfishes, brittle stars, sea urchins, sand dollars, sea lilies, and sea cucumbers, all are marine. Some live near the shore, others at depths of up to two miles (3.2 km). Like the coelenterates they have radial symmetry, their arms or other structures radiating from the center like spokes in a wheel. Echinoderms move by tubefeet that line the grooves in their arms, each "foot" ending in a suction cup. A bulb at the opposite end pumps water out of the foot to create the suction, and the hold is released by pumping water into the foot again. The only animals in this group that are dangerous to the touch are sea urchins—though starfishes, sea cucumbers, and some others contain poisons in their bodies.

Sea Urchins *(Diadema, Adrosoma, etc.)*

Sea urchins have a globular shell that encases their body. The shell consists of five closely fitting plates with grooves between them on the underside. These plates are complements of a starfish's arms. In the center of the undersurface is the mouth, which bears five white teeth. This chewing mechanism is called Aristotle's lantern because when it is detached from the skeleton, it looks like a type of oil lantern used years ago.

Most sea urchins measure two or three inches (5–7.6 cm) across their shell, though their size ranges from less than half an inch (12 mm) to more than a foot (30 cm). Their shell is covered with spines, each independently movable and used for locomotion. Some sea urchins use their spines to burrow in the sand or mud or in soft, limy rocks; others use them to spike their way up pilings. Some have small spines, others have very large ones—to ten inches (25 cm) or more in a sea urchin that lives in the South Pacific. The big spines are collected and **109**

▲ Long-spined sea urchin ▼ Red sea urchin (entire animal)

used like pencils for writing on slate. In many species, the spines are as sharp as needles. If a sea urchin is stepped on, its brittle spines can pierce deeply into the foot and then break off. Removing the spines is difficult, even if they have not penetrated very far. Secondary infections are distinctly a danger. The hollow spines of some are filled with venom, used by the animals strictly for defense. Human deaths have been reported though not confirmed.

Scattered among the spines over their body, sea urchins also have little pincer organs, or pedicellariae. These are used principally to keep the body cleaned of any small animals that might attach themselves to the sea urchin's shell. The pedicellariae of some sea urchins are equipped to inject venom. The amount released is minute, but it can be bothersome, resembling a bee sting. The stings from a large number of these tiny jaws can result in a general numbness, difficulty in breathing, and even death.

▲ Pencil sea urchin

Sharks, Rays, and Ratfishes
These are the most primitive of the animals with backbones, but their skeletons consist of cartilage rather than bone. Sharks are mostly streamlined creatures and are feared because of their bites. Most sharks are not poisonous. Rays are flat-bodied bottom dwellers, and in contrast to sharks, many are equipped with poisonous spines. The ratfishes, or chimaeras, generally inhabit deep waters and are intermediate between bony fishes and the sharks and rays. All ratfishes have a venomous spine **112** on their dorsal fin, using it as protection from attackers.

▲ Spiny dogfish

Spiny Dogfish (*Squalus acanthias*)

The spiny dogfish is a shark that lives in the cool waters of both the Atlantic and the Pacific, sometimes occurring in great numbers. It averages less than three feet (91 cm) in length, with occasional individuals to five feet (1.5 m) long. The spiny dogfish has the annoying habit of stealing baits or helping itself also to fish already hooked. Many are caught in the nets of commercial fishermen. In Europe they are sold as food.

In front of each of the spiny dogfish's two dorsal fins is a sharp spine, and it seems to be almost impossible to get one of these squirming sharks off a hook or out of a net without being impaled by a spine. At the base of each spine is a venom gland that sends a mild toxin down the grooved spine and into the wound. Both the spine and the venom are used strictly for defense. The poison causes great pain and swelling, which may last for as long as a week. Deaths from these stab wounds have been reported but are not officially documented. Great care should be exercised with these little sharks, however.

Stingrays (Family Dasyatidae)

Stingrays form a distinct family among the flat, bottom-dwelling rays. They feed mainly on mollusks but may also eat crustaceans, fish, or other small animals. All have a long, whiplike tail that has on each side of its base one or several spines with poison glands. When a spine impales a victim, the poison runs down a groove in the spine and into the wound. The pain is immediate, throbbing, and excruciating. In most cases, the wounds are inflicted on a person's feet or legs as a result of stepping on the stingrays when wading. The stingrays lash their tails and imbed their barbed spines as a defense mechanism. They do not attack. The spines may rip gashes as long as six inches (15 cm). Occasionally when a wound occurs on the chest, neck, or arms—usually a result of trying to handle the rays—deaths have resulted. Secondary infection, the most dangerous being tetanus, is also a hazard. It is impor-   **113**

▲ Yellow-spotted stingray ▼ Eagle ray

tant to get medical attention immediately. Because stingrays are so often found in shallow water and especially in beach areas, they are responsible for more injuries to humans than are any other fishes. They should be avoided, and when wading, it is important to shuffle the feet along the bottom to scare off rays that may be ahead. Often a school of literally thousands of rays will move into a beach area and pave the bottom with their bodies.

About a hundred species of stingrays occur in warm, shallow seas around the world, and some wander into brackish and even fresh waters. Most measure less than a foot (30 cm) across their wings, but a few have spans exceeding six feet (1.8 m). Included in the stingray family are the handsome butterfly rays (*Gymnura marmorata*) with pointed ''wings'' that are the same size or greater than the length of the ray's body. Butterfly rays are more active than most stingrays. The spines at the base of their tail are short and not highly effective as weapons.

Eagle rays *(Aetobatus narinari),* less commonly seen in shallow waters than butterfly rays, feed actively in the open water, as the great mantas do. Some measure as much as eight feet (2.4 m) across their wings, and they may weigh more than 500 pounds (227 kg). These big rays are not usually encountered by swimmers or divers, but they do have one or several short, sharp spines at the base of their tail. It is difficult for the ray to use them even in self-defense.

Ratfishes or Chimaeras *(Chimaera, Hydrolagus)*
Ratfishes generally live in cool, deep waters, to a depth of a mile and a half (2.4 km) or more. A few occur in surface waters, and they are not uncommon catches on baited hooks. All have a large, sharp serrated spine, used only in self-defense when the fish is handled, at the front of the first dorsal fin. At the base of the spine are venom glands that produce toxin. If the spine pierces the skin, it causes great pain and swelling. No deaths due to stings have been reported, however. **115**

Bony Fishes

These are the most abundant, most successful, and most familiar fishes. More than 20,000 species inhabit the waters of the
world. They are more advanced than sharks and rays because
they have skeletons of bone rather than of cartilage, a single
cover (the operculum) for their gills, scales that completely
cover their body (some bony fish totally lack them, however),
and spines that strengthen their fins. Bony fishes occur in a
great variety of sizes and shapes and are equally diversified in
their habits and habitats. Only a few species produce
venom—which is truly astonishing in such a large group of
116 animals.

▲ Ratfish

Weeverfishes *(Trachinus draco, T. vipera, T. radiatus,* and *T. araneus)*

These are the most dangerous of all the venomous fishes that live in cool marine waters. Three species occur off the coasts of Europe and Africa, and one is found off the coast of Chile in South America. These fish are particularly dangerous because of their habit of burying themselves in the sand along beaches, where they are easily stepped on. They are also commonly caught in nets by commercial fishermen, and the great weever, which grows to nearly 1½ feet (46 cm) long, is harvested as food in Europe.

Weevers are slim fish, their ventral and pectoral fins located far forward (under their throat). Their anal and second dorsal fins are very long. Their venom is contained in the long spine of the first dorsal fin and also in the long spine on each gill cover. Like most snake venoms, the toxin is complex, including both neurotoxic and hemotoxic elements. The pain is severe and spreads rapidly, reaching its peak within about half an hour and lasting for as long as a day. Recovery may require several months, particularly if secondary infections develop.

▲ Lesser weeverfish

Scorpionfishes (Family Scorpaenidae)

The scorpionfishes include the most venomous of all the fish in the sea. The family contains about 300 species that occur in seas around the world. Not all of the species produce a venom, but all are spiny and can inflict deep and painful wounds that are slow in healing. Their spines and venom are strictly for defense. Most members of the family live in deep, rocky waters that are close to shore. They are often caught on hook and line. Some, such as the blue rockfish found off the coast of California, are sought after by sport fishermen; others are caught commercially and are sold as ocean perch. Various species of scorpionfishes are encountered by divers, and a few are aggressive, attacking almost any moving object. In all, the venom is produced by glands located in their grooved spines on the dorsal, anal, and ventral fins. Only the most common and dangerous of the scorpionfishes are described here.

Deadly Stonefish *(Synaceja horrida, S. trachynis,* and *S. verrucosa)* live in the Indo-Pacific waters. The venom glands in their short, thick spines are extraordinarily long and bulbous. Ugly, warty, and brownish black, a perfect disguise in the debris in which they hide, the sluggish stonefish is difficult to see and therefore avoid. It grows to a foot (30 cm) long but is usually shorter. The stab wounds from its spines are extremely painful, the pain and swelling spreading rapidly. Deaths are not uncommon and have occurred in as short a time as two hours after a sting. Even if a victim does not get a lethal dosage, his recovery may require many months.

Zebrafish *(Pteroris volitans)* inhabit warm Pacific waters and coral reefs. It is handsomely striped with black and white or other colors, the rays of its fins generally drawn out into thin filaments. This beautiful fish, about six inches (15 cm) long, is **119**

◀ Scorpionfish ▲ Stonefish

▲ Lionfish ▼ Stinging catfish

less deadly than the stonefish but is nevertheless quite dangerous. Its bright colors make it easier to see, but its attractiveness
lures some divers into catching it, not difficult to do because
the zebrafish swims in the open and moves rather slowly. The
zebrafish goes also by such names as lionfish, turkeyfish,
butterflyfish, and stingfish.

Scorpionfish or Lionfish (Scorpaena, Centropogon, Scor-
paenopsis, Choridactylus, and others) are a large group of
venomous scorpionfishes. The California sculpin (Scorpaena
guttata), for example, is found from central California southward into Mexican waters. All are poisonous, some nearly as
dangerous as zebrafishes.

Catfishes (Galeichthys, Heteropneustes, Plotosus, Bagre, and others)
Fish that comprise more than a dozen families are known
collectively as catfish. Most of them live in freshwaters, but
some are marine. Some are less than three inches (8 cm) long
when full grown and are popular as aquarium fish, primarily
because they are scavengers that help keep the aquarium
clean. Others are among the largest of all fishes, weighing
hundreds of pounds. Most of the catfishes are ''naked,'' or
scaleless, but some kinds wear an armor of heavy, fused
scales. Typically, catfishes have a broad, flat head, small eyes,
and chin whiskers (barbels). They also have sharp spines in
both their first dorsal and their pectoral fins. In many species
the spines are equipped with tiny teeth or serrations, and some
kinds have venomous glands at the base of the spines. The
toxin is not lethal (except possibly one freshwater species in
South America), but it is powerful enough to make the wound
throb with pain and swell. The more venomous species are
found in Indo-Pacific waters, but the common sea catfish
along the Atlantic coast of North America apparently produces a mild venom. The stab wounds of these spines are
probably more dangerous because of the possibility of secondary infection rather than because of the venom. **121**

▲ Common sea catfish ▼ Toadfish

Toadfishes (Family Batrachoididae)

These small bottom-dwelling fishes (about three dozen species) are common in temperate to warm waters throughout the world. Typically they hide in debris and then dart out of hiding to catch their prey. Like toads, they are wide-mouthed and big-eyed, and they also make toadlike croaking noises. Those that live in shallow waters are easily stepped on by waders. Toadfishes, most of them less than a foot long, are often caught, too, on baits and lures. Most of the species are not venomous, but those living in tropical waters and in the Indo-Pacific region and in tropical America have poison glands that release venom through the first two spines of the dorsal fins and through the spine on each of the gill covers. These spines are hollow. Toadfishes are not deadly, but the mild venom injected into their stab wounds causes immediate and great pain.

Electric Stargazers (Uranoscopus scaber)

Electric stargazers (see page 84) pack two punches—stunning blows of electricity and also a venom. This poison is potent enough not only to cause great pain and discomfort, but also (in some species, such as the European stargazer) to kill a human.

123

▲ Yellowfin toadfish

Rabbitfishes (Family Siganidae)

So-named because of the rabbitlike appearance of their mouth, the 20 species or so of rabbitfishes live in the tropical waters of the Indo-Pacific. Almost all are herbivorous, grazing on plants close to shore. All of the spines in their fins are grooved and contain venom glands in the outer third of their length. Stab wounds are painful, the wounds healing slowly. In the usual small amounts received, the poison is not lethal.

Surgeonfishes (Family Acanthuridae)

Surgeonfishes are close relatives of rabbitfishes but belong to a different family. About a hundred species inhabit coral reef waters around the world. The typical surgeonfishes have one or more sharp, knifelike spine at each side of the caudal peduncle. These are usually kept folded into grooves, but they **124** are lifted when the fish becomes disturbed and used as weap-

▲ Yellow surgeonfish with sharp "knives"
(on each side of tail) that can be used as weapons

ons of defense, making deep, slashing wounds. Some species may also inject a venom into the wound.

Dragonets (Family Callionymidae)

Dragonets are small bottom-dwelling fishes that live in temperate and tropical waters. They have a sharp and possibly venomous hooked spine on each gill opening, located on top of the head. Best known is the European dragonet *(Callionymus lyra)*, which reaches a length of about eight inches (20 cm). In the breeding season—spring to summer—the males become brightly colored.

Other fishes are suspected of being venomous, none lethal but possibly producing mild poisons that are transmitted to wounds made by their spines. Unless you know the species of a fish positively, it is wise to handle it with caution. **125**

▲ Surgeonfish

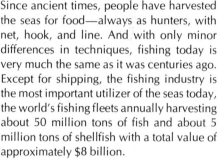

Poisonous to Eat

Since ancient times, people have harvested the seas for food—always as hunters, with net, hook, and line. And with only minor differences in techniques, fishing today is very much the same as it was centuries ago. Except for shipping, the fishing industry is the most important utilizer of the seas today, the world's fishing fleets annually harvesting about 50 million tons of fish and about 5 million tons of shellfish with a total value of approximately $8 billion.

But even more harvests are needed to provide the protein needed by the world's burgeoning population. Of the some 20,000 species of fish in the seas, we now use only a few dozen. We must learn to use many other kinds. Those that are not particularly flavorful but that are nevertheless abundant and nutritious—the so-called "trash" fish—can be turned into fish flours and meals. Called FPC (fish protein concentrate) or MPC (marine protein concentrate), this fine-grained flour is tasteless and odorless. Added to breads, soups, cereals, and other foods, the highly concentrated protein flour, which averages seventy-five percent protein but may be as high as eighty-five percent, can supply a normal person's total protein needs for only a few cents per day. The grayish **127**

◄ Green sea turtle

powder keeps without spoilage with no refrigeration.

Spoilage, in fact, has been one of the major problems of fish for consumption. Some kinds begin to deteriorate almost as soon as they are removed from the water, and few kinds can be kept long without some sort of preservation. Truly fresh fish is almost odorless, quite unlike the fishy smell that identifies most fish markets. While quick freezing has made it possible to harvest fish that are found far from land without immediately returning to port, the frozen fish do not have the delicate flavor that makes fresh-caught fish so pleasing to the palate. Preservation—by refrigeration, freezing, canning, smoking, salting, or some other method—is essential for preventing illness caused by eating spoiled fish. This kind of poisoning is the result of bacteria of decay that become rampant in fish as soon as its fats and oils begin to deteriorate.

Fish also harbor many kinds of parasites, both external and internal. A fish with warty growths on its body does not look at all appetizing, though most of these external parasites are not

▲ Atlantic jackknife clam

dangerous to humans and will not even reinfest if they are not destroyed. This is also true of most kinds of internal parasites, even those that are not visible to the naked eye and that are eaten unknowingly along with the fish. Except for those kinds that are protected in cysts, internal parasites are killed in cooking. Some are even eaten knowingly in countries where ''fish with macaroni (worms)'' are intentionally served.

But there are some kinds of tapeworms and other flatworms in fish that reinfest humans. If the fish are heated to a high enough temperature in cooking, most of these worms are **129**

▲ Mussels

destroyed. In some countries, however, raw fish are popular, which, of course, increases the risk of infestation. It is advisable to inspect fish carefully and to cut out all of the cysts or other evidences of parasites, and it is also safest to cook the fish before eating it.

Still other kinds of fish and shellfish are poisonous because they contain toxic substances that they have acquired from the animals they eat. The symptoms of fish poisoning, which cannot be detected in the taste of the fish, are generally similar: intestinal pain, vomiting, diarrhea, and a general weakness. In mild cases, recovery is quick—within at least a few days—but in some kinds of poisoning, the recovery may require months or even years.

Clams, Mussels, and Other Mollusks

Clams, mussels, oysters, and their kin are filter feeders. They get their food from water currents and so they must take whatever comes to them. In most areas, the plankton on which they feed is harmless, but there are places and times when the sea swarms with tiny poisonous dinoflagellates, which are mobile marine one-celled algae. From these, the shellfish **130** accumulate large amounts of the poison in their bodies and

▲ Common cockle

are poisonous to eat, though curiously they are not affected by the poison themselves. The "red tides" along Florida's Gulf Coast are due to dinoflagellates.

"Mussel poisoning" from eating mussels harvested off the California coast and northward to Alaska originates in this manner. When there are "blooms" of poisonous dinoflagellates—usually in the warm months—the beaches are posted to warn people not to harvest the shellfish. Deaths have been recorded from eating the poisoned shellfish during these times. Many years ago, coastal Indians recognized the deadliness of shellfish at some times of the year, and they warned Indians from inland areas not to eat the shellfish.

▲ Butter clam, or smooth Washington

Shellfish poisoning is not confined to North America. It is also known to occur off the coasts of Africa, New Zealand, Australia, Canada, and northern Europe. No antidotes for the poison have been developed. If poisoning is suspected, it is important to get all of the poison out of the intestinal tract immediately by inducing vomiting. This type of poisoning does not cause nausea—the victim experiences a general weakness, aching, and dizziness followed by paralysis and eventually death if the dosage has been large. There is no reliable way, either, of determining which shellfish are poisonous by either their appearance or odor. A thorough washing will help to flush out concentrations of the poisonous dinoflagellates but does not guarantee that all have been eliminated. No shellfish should be taken from an area under quarantine.

Fish that are Poisonous

Most kinds of poisonous fish—and the list includes several hundred species—inhabit warm waters, especially coral reef waters. These are fish that are poisonous when eaten fresh. They are toxic primarily because of a buildup of poisons from the foods they eat. Some may not be poisonous at all times of the year. In some kinds, the poison is concentrated in the internal organs, but in others it occurs throughout the body. Only the most common poisonous fish are described here.

Sharks

Most sharks are good to eat, though they are not generally popular in the United States, but throughout Europe and Asia most sharks and many rays are rated as delicious fare. Some are eaten fresh, but because they tend to spoil quickly, they are usually preserved by smoking, salting, or canning soon after they are caught. A few kinds do have records for being poisonous, however.

The Greenland shark *(Somniosus microcephalus)*, which

▲ Great white shark ▼ Black-tipped shark

may weigh a ton and measure to 24 feet (7.3 m) in length, inhabits arctic waters. Unbelievably sluggish and unwary, the Greenland shark is easily caught on hook and line or harpooned, and it is eaten regularly by Eskimos and others who depend on the cold waters to supply their food. They have learned from experience that this shark is poisonous and that it must be cooked in several waters before it is safe for eating. It is generally also dried before it is consumed. The effect of the toxin is unusual, producing hallucinations and other nervous disorders. This occurs also in dogs that are fed the raw flesh of the Greenland shark. Deaths have been recorded.

Most poisonings due to eating sharks have occurred in the subtropics or tropics, and among the species said to be responsible are the great hammerhead shark, six-gilled shark, seven-gilled shark, black-tipped shark, and white shark. Most of the reports are not authenticated. It is believed that the taboos against eating sharks result from the fact that sharks do occasionally eat humans rather than from the fear of poisoning. The most severe poisonings, resulting from eating the livers, commence with nausea and a general aching within

about half an hour followed by loss of coordination and ability

▲ Seven-gilled shark

to breathe. No antidotes have been developed, though drugs may be used to alleviate some of the discomfort. If a sufficient amount of poison is ingested, death results. For these obvious reasons, the liver or other visceral parts of sharks should not be eaten, and the flesh of tropical sharks should be consumed with caution.

Moray Eels

Moray eels, not related to the highly edible freshwater eels, inhabit subtrobical and tropical waters throughout the world and are especially abundant in coral reefs. Many species are large, attaining lengths of ten feet (3 m), and they also have thick, meaty bodies. Some are good to eat, but about half a dozen species have been identified as poisonous. All are from tropical seas. The flesh of these eels is poisonous, and in the Pacific it is often prepared in the most dangerous way—as eel

▲ Moray eel

soup, a thick broth made primarily from the blood. Since the toxin is soluble, the soup contains a strong concentration of poison. A victim of moray eel poisoning first experiences nausea, but as the poisoning progresses, his nervous system is also affected and he has convulsions and difficulty in breathing. Only about one out of ten persons dies, but the recovery of those that do survive is extremely slow, sometimes requiring a year or longer.

Tunas

Tunas, mackerels, bonitos, and their relatives are among the tastiest of all the fishes of the seas and are much sought after by both sport and commercial fishermen. Under normal circumstances they are not poisonous, but they are also among those kinds of fish that must be eaten or preserved soon after they are caught. These fast-swimming fish have a high metabolism rate, and immediately after they die, their rich blood starts a chemical breakdown. Within a few hours, they are contaminated with a histaminelike compound that produces an allergic reaction in those who eat the flesh—starting with stomach pains, vomiting, diarrhea, and culminating with a rash of welts over the body. Deaths have been reported.

If a fish of this group is suspected of being less than fresh, which is generally easy to determine by its odor and appearance (sunken eyes, gills no longer red), it should be thrown away. Or if there is a sharp or biting taste to the flesh of a fish that has been cooked, no more should be eaten.

Puffers

Puffers or blowfish (family Tetraodontidae and Centhigasteridae) and some of their relatives (porcupinefishes and ocean sunfishes) include the most poisonous to eat of all fishes in the sea. They are found in temperate to tropical seas throughout the world, occurring most abundantly in warm
136 waters. The degree of toxicity of these fish may vary from

Deadly death puffer ▲ Pacific bonitos ▼

season to season but appears to be greatest at spawning time, with a concentration of the poison in the fish's gonads. The poison (tetrodotoxin) is so powerful and quick-acting that deaths sometimes occur within only fifteen minutes after some of the fish has been eaten. The death rate from the poisoning exceeds fifty percent, and there is no known antidote. Many people are saved because they detect the effects of the quick-acting poisoning before they have eaten large amounts of the fish. The Japanese have used puffers for committing suicide.

The deadly toxin may be found anywhere in the fish's body but is usually concentrated in the internal organs. In Japan, **137** where puffers are rated as a delicacy called *fugu*, the government licenses special cooks who are trained in the art of preparing puffers so that they can be eaten without danger of poisoning. The art consists essentially of an extremely careful cleaning so that the viscera are not permitted to contact and contaminate the flesh. But even these experts make mistakes, and unfortunately puffer poisoning occurs regularly in Japan. Despite the reputation of these fish for being flavorful, no puffers or any of their relatives should be given a place on your plate. The chances of poisoning are too great.

Ciguatera

Throughout the subtropics and tropics, there are hundreds of species of fish that produce, at times, a poisoning called ciguatera. Most of these fish are predators. The poisons in their bodies are derived from the foods they eat, reaching high levels by the process of accumulation or biological magnification (in the same manner that DDT and other insecticides reach lethal levels in animals at the top of food pyramids). It is also probable that the poison results from a chemical reaction in the fish and that the original food was not at all poisonous.

Ciguatera or "fish poisoning" may suddenly appear in an area where it has not been known previously, or a species may be edible in one area but poisonous when taken from waters only a short distance away. In some cases the young of a species are not poisonous, but the full-grown or mature individuals may be highly dangerous, indicating that the toxins build up over long periods of time. The toxicity of a species may also change from season to season. Ciguatera occurs also in varying degrees of intensity, but in all cases it affects the nervous system of a victim, causing paralysis or semiparalysis. It is fatal in only slightly more than five percent of the cases, but complete recovery may require many months or even years.

So many species of fish have been implicated in ciguatera in the subtropics and tropics that to name them all would neces-

Spotted puffer ▶

sitate providing extensive checklists for each area. Among the most familiar, however, are the barracudas, considered by many to be among the tastiest of all fish. In Florida, for example, they were once sold in large numbers in markets under the name of "gray sea bass," but cases of ciguatera made it necessary to ban their sale. About a dozen species of snappers and as many kinds of sea basses—both popular food fish— have been known to be poisonous. The ladyfish, popular with sport fishermen, is known to be poisonous, too, but is rarely eaten. As a precaution, never eat the roe, liver, or other internal organs of any fish, for if the fish is at all toxic, the poison will be concentrated here. If there are warnings about particular species in an area, heed them. There is no way to determine by its looks that a fish is poisonous. If after a fish is eaten, one develops symptoms of poisoning, immediately induce vomiting to get rid of whatever still remains in the digestive tract. Get medical attention immediately.

Sea Turtles

Turtles are considered one of the finest delicacies of all the foods from the sea. The green turtles of the Caribbean have a flavor much like veal, for example. In this region, the turtles' diet consists almost wholly of turtle grass. But in the Indo-Pacific region, the green turtle as well as other sea turtles are not uncommonly poisonous. Here they do not have the vast pastures of plants on which to forage, and they join the others of their clan in subsisting on animals. Included in their diets are jellyfish, and over a period of time the toxins from the jellyfish or other creatures build up in their systems to a level that makes them dangerous to eat. As in the case of shellfish and fish, make careful checks before assuming that a turtle is edible.

▲ Green sea turtle

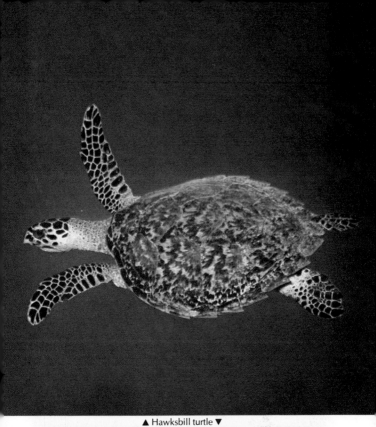

▲ Hawksbill turtle ▼

141

Killer Whales and Other Mammals

8

Mammals are basically land dwellers, but a few groups have become aquatic or semi-aquatic. The most completely adapted for life in water are the cetaceans (whales, dolphins, and porpoises), their bodies streamlined like a fish's and their front legs modified into flippers for swimming (hind legs lacking). But despite their fishlike appearance, all cetaceans must surface periodically to breath air, as must also the walruses, seals, and sea lions, which belong to the same order of mammals as dogs and cats (Order Carnivora).

Killer Whales *(Orcinus orca)*

A killer whale, or grampus, could easily kill a human if it wished. It has long been ranked as the most ferocious and voracious of all animals on land or in the sea, more feared than sharks. But despite this reputation and its unquestioned capabilities, the killer whale has never attacked a human—or at least there are no verified records. To the contrary, man is the killer whale's enemy, and the only enemy it has. This is not a recommendation to welcome a killer whale. The killer whale is indeed a fearsome beast, and while it has a clean record at the moment, there is always that chance that some **143**

◄ Killer whale

rogue may spoil it. Killer whales are not to be played with unless you are an expert.

The killer whale is the largest of all the dolphins, a family (Delphinidae) of principally small-toothed whales, and is easily identified by its striking black-and-white coloration. A male killer whale may measure 30 feet long (9 m), the female at least a third smaller. The dorsal fin is very large—up to six feet in older animals—and protrudes from the water as the killer speeds along near the surface. It has been clocked at 30 miles (48 km) per hour in the open ocean! The front flippers are large and bluntly rounded across their tips, and the tail flukes are broad, fleshy horizontal extensions.

Like other dolphins and whales, the killer whale is a warmblooded, air-breathing mammal whose ancestors deserted the land and returned to the sea. They are the best-adapted mammals for aquatic life. Except for a few bristles, they lack hair. Beneath the skin they have a thick layer of blubber, or fat, that insulates their body and holds in heat. They breathe through a "blowhole" on top of their head, and this opening can be tightly closed for submerging.

The killer whale roams oceans throughout the world but is most common in cold polar seas. Often it appears along coasts. Traveling in packs (pods) of a few to as many as 40 or 50 animals, they work together in herding and harassing their victim until it is exhausted, and then they move in to make the kill. Sharks, seals, penguins, dolphins, whales—no animal in the sea can escape a hungry, prowling pod of killer whales, and their slaughter often exceeds their needs. There are reports of killer whales attacking and killing giant blue whales and then wastefully consuming only the tongue. They consume large quantities of fish and squid, which probably constitute a major portion of their diet. The killer whale has about 40 conical teeth with which it holds its prey and uses to bite off big chunks. It uses its big pink tongue to help it in holding food.

Exploding the many myths about its viciousness, this giant

beast has in recent years proved to be rather easily tamed. It rivals other dolphins in its response to training and becomes quite docile in captivity. Several marine exhibits now feature killer whales among their star attractions and performers. Like other dolphins, the killer whales have a ''language'' that they use in communicating among themselves, and they demonstrate a remarkable interest in coming to each other's aid.

To man, the killer whale should surely be considered friendly rather than dangerous. It has been included here to call attention to the fact that there has been a reversal of what was believed about killer whales in the past. But the killer whale is also a Goliath that should not be underestimated. If you do find yourself sharing the sea with one or several killer whales, it is most advisable to relinquish the space for the moment—and be grateful that these monstrous animals are kinder to man than he has been to them.

▲ Northern fur seal

Walruses, Seals, and Sea Lions

Closely related carnivores (bears, dogs, cats, and other flesh-eaters), these marine mammals are so well adapted for aquatic life that they can move on land only clumsily. Their stream-lined bodies, flipperlike feet, and webbed toes make swimming easy for them. Their tail is very short. Some have small external ears; others none. They are not, however, as totally adapted to an aquatic existence as are whales and dolphins. They must return to land (or ice) to give birth to their young and to care for them until they are old enough to take to the sea. A thick layer of blubber insulates them from the cold water.

Walruses, seals, and sea lions are found in all seas through-**146** out the world except in the northern part of the Indian Ocean.

▲ Walrus *(Odobenus rosmarus)*

They are most abundant in the cold polar seas. Men have
hunted them since before written history. Their thick fur made
warm clothes and shelter; their rich meat stoked hungry
stomachs and provided the fuel for inner warmth in the cold.
Their bones and teeth were carved into implements and or-
naments. The small number of people who lived near enough
to harvest these animals for such personal needs took all they
could use without damaging the total population. But when
great schooners ventured into the waters and began hauling
meat and hides to ports around the world, slaughtering half a
million or more animals every year, the population of seals
began to dwindle alarmingly. Governments now control the
number that can be harvested annually. **147**

▲ Sea lion ▼ Leopard seal

Because most of these mammals survive in remote areas, the chances of people encountering them in the wild are slim. In addition, they are ordinarily neither mean nor aggressive. Except for a possible flaring of temper in an individual when molested, the only danger is during the breeding season when these animals come ashore on islands or on some coasts to breed and rear their young. At this time the bulls or big males—which in the Pribilof, or Alaskan, fur seal *(Callorhinus alascanus)* may weigh 700 pounds (317 kg); a bull walrus **148** *(Odobenus rosmarus)*, to 1.5 tons (1.3 M tons)—establish

territories in which they maintain harems. All during the breeding season, the bulls do not eat, not daring to take off time from the round-the-clock guard of their harem against invasion by other bulls. But any other invader may be chased, too, as inquisitive humans (usually equipped with cameras) have discovered. There are reports, too, of attacks on boats by female animals with young. Many animals become highly sensitive during the breeding season and when rearing their young, and they should be allowed complete privacy at these times.

▲ Bull sea lion

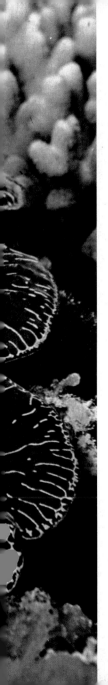

Dangerous by Accident

9

In the sea as on land, few creatures really attack humans, and when they do it is generally in self-defense rather than with malicious intent. Mankind invades and provokes in a world that is not his domain. Most of the creatures described earlier in this book are specifically equipped to take care of themselves against trespassers, using teeth, spines, and venoms to protect their rights. Others may be dangerous even though they lack such devices, doing harm by accident, but nevertheless acquiring unjustified reputations as fearsome beasts.

A few of the dangers of this sort are described here, such as the myth of a man-eating clam. This is only a sampling, of course, for accidents of this sort might occur anywhere. They are mistakes, but some are avoidable if there is an awareness to the danger.

Tridacna Clam *(Tridacna gigas)*
One of the beauties of nature, this giant among all bivalved mollusks is found on Australia's Great Barrier Reef and throughout the Indo-Pacific region. Once a clam has completed its larval growth, it settles on the sea floor and never moves again. Full grown, it may weigh 500 pounds (227 kg) and mea- **151**

◀ Tridacna clam

sure five feet (1.5 m) across its massive shells. The soft living animals inside the shells weigh only 20 to 25 pounds (9–11 kg), however. The big clam harbors colonies of green algae in the soft mantle that lines the fluted shell and curtains its gills. These provide the clam with its food, for to get its meals the clam needs only to spread this mantle in the sunlight and allow the tiny green plants to proliferate. The clam subsists on the surplus produced by this convenient built-in food factory. Pearls larger than golf balls have been found inside the giant clam's shell, but they have no value. Islanders use sharp pieces of the shell to make tools and weapons.

Many tales are told about divers that have been caught in the powerful grip of a giant clam's shell. Whether any of the stories are true is not known, but they seem highly unlikely. First of all, most of these big clams live in very shallow and clear water. They are quite visible and avoidable, and since their shells stand two or three (16–91 cm) feet high, it would take a bit of doing to climb into one. Further, the great shell does not snap shut but closes slowly so that anyone realizing his mistake could get out before being caught. In the case of clams found in deeper water, it is more conceivable that an accident might occur, but there are no authenticated records of such a tragedy ever really happening—only the persistent legends embellished with every imaginable horror adjective. The giant clam is definitely not a man-eater or a killer that lies in wait for human victims.

▲ Tridacna clam

Living Javelins

Freakish accidents of many kinds might be related, but a few are to a degree predictable because they are repeated time after time. In subtropical and tropical waters, for example, there are about 50 species of needlefishes *(Strongylura),* close relatives of the flyingfishes and halfbeaks. Most needlefish are less than two feet long, but a few are as much as twice as long and may weigh to 12 pounds. They are slim-bodied, and their jaws are needlelike, forming a long, sharp beak. Most of the needlefish live in waters close to shore, and they swim close to the surface. When excited, they have a habit of leaping into the air, hurtling through space like spears or arrows. At night they are attracted to lights and will leap toward them. Fishermen with lights in their boats after dark have been struck by these missiles. Several deaths are recorded resulting from such accidents, the needlefish puncturing the victim's neck and major blood vessels. There have been numerous instances in which victims have narrowly escaped being blinded when struck near an eye. One man was impaled through the leg by a needlefish and pinned to his boat. Knowing that needlefish are a potential danger, the wise fisherman does not set himself up as a target. He uses his light as little as possible and shields it so that it does not attract the fish.

153

▲ Needlefish

Blunderers

A few years ago off Fort Myers Beach in Florida, a woman was sunbathing on the afterdeck of a cruiser while her husband was fishing off the bow. Suddenly a giant eagle ray weighing several hundred pounds rocketed skyward from the calm bay waters. Its vertical leap spent, the monster dropped flatly back toward the sea, but by accident it was now directly over the cruiser. The woman was jolted from her rest by the big ray, which floundered on top of her. When the incident was over, the ray hung at the dock, having paid with death for its mistake. The woman was in the hospital with two broken legs and a bad case of shock, vowing never again to set out to sea.

Other rays have caused injuries by accident, flailing their powerful "wings" when they have been beached or boated. Some, including even the giant mantas, have cut divers' air lines with their "wings" when they have come to investigate **154** the rising bubbles.

▲ Eagle ray

Sharks have been responsible for similar kinds of accidents. The otherwise harmless and sluggish basking shark, for example, is not infrequently trapped in the nets of commercial fishermen, and because of its great size, the shark may destroy the nets and even smash fishing boats in making its escape. The basking shark is one of the few that has also been accused of being aggressive—that is, ramming boats or leaping out of the water and then intentionally coming down on top of boats. But declaring the shark's intentions is just man's interpretation. Most incidents of this nature are accidents, some of them avoidable.

It should always be kept in mind that any giant fish packs great power in its lashing tail. The fish may intend only to get away, but if a fisherman or his boat gets in the path of the mighty tail, a tragedy could occur. No matter what the circumstance, people are too fragile to compete with such mighty opponents.

Poor Sports

Catching a big one is great sport for the fisherman—but not the fish. And big fish sometimes get this point across quite clearly. The tarpon, which regularly reaches a weight of 25 to 50 pounds (11.3–22.6 kg) and is known to weigh as much as 300 pounds (136 kg), is sometimes called ''the poor man's big game fish.'' It lives close to shore and can be fished for off bridges or jetties and from skiffs. Big ocean-going boats and expensive gear are not essential for catching tarpon. Once hooked, a tarpon becomes pure dynamite, exploding from the water in skyward leaps and then plunging back again. Time after time the tarpon performs, and with each surging leap, it shakes itself furiously to try and throw the hook. Not infrequently it succeeds! The hook and sinker then fly through the air with bulletlike speed, and the fisherman himself, if he is keeping a tight line, helps direct them. He may recover consciousness to discover that he was hit directly between the **155**

eyes by the lead weight on his line, or he may discover that the thrown hook is now barb-deep in his arm, shoulder, or neck. And out there in the water the tarpon still leaps but is scot-free.

If a tarpon is not successful in throwing the hook, then the fisherman is in for a long battle if he wants to boat his quarry. Lacking the gimbals or a fighting chair that is usually on a big-game fishing boat, he tackles the tarpon bare armed, his rod supported in the crook of his elbow. When he feels the strength of the fish's lunges and sees its shimmering silvery body above the blue waters he forgets about the incredible pressure against his arm. Tarpon fishermen have been known to ignore the loss of circulation of blood for such an extended period that they have lost the use of their arm permanently, all for the sake of a fish.

Nor is the danger over when at last the fish tires and is secured inside the boat. Sometimes after a short rest and inspired by a need for oxygen, the tarpon may suddenly come to life again. Its thrashing can not only wreck the cockpit but also break an arm or a leg. People should remember that very few animals succumb without a violent struggle, and when a **156** fish is large and powerful, its struggles can indeed be violent.

▲ Tarpon

All big fish, whether tarpons or other species, can do physical harm simply because of their size. They must be treated with caution. And any fish, no matter what its size, must be handled with care because of its incidental but highly effective weaponry. Many marine fish have razor-sharp gill covers that can make a slashing wound if a fisherman makes the mistake of trying to pick them up by running his hand into the gills. Even small fish can be dangerous in this manner. Most also have sharp spines in their fins, and if a fish is grasped across the back without a firm grip, it can rip its way free, leaving a bloody hand. Wounds of this sort are usually not deep or serious in themselves but are often ignored, which is the greatest danger. Then, either directly from the fish or from elsewhere after the incident, the cuts are likely to spawn secondary infections that can indeed be bad. Tetanus, of course, is the greatest of the hazards.

Dirty Beaches

Beaches are littered with ocean debris. In this litter, people find many treasures cast up by the sea, and scavenging the beaches after storms is especially productive for shell hunters. But beachcombing has its hazards, too. In the mats of seaweed there may be strands of broken tentacles from jellyfish or from a Portuguese man-o-war. Even detached from the body, these threads still contain nematocysts that can fire their harpoons and inject venom. Similarly fire corals are tossed onto the beaches, or beneath a shell there may be a frightened little octopus with a venomous bite that can kill a person. Broken off in the sand and buried just out of sight, there may be a jagged edge of a pen shell turned up so that it can easily slice into a foot. Yes, the dangers of the sea do sometimes wash ashore. But alertness is a safeguard.

The most dangerous of all, however, is the litter left by humans. Bottles, cans, hooks, pollution...mankind's debris in sea is far more dangerous than its creatures. **157**

Index

Marc Ziliox was born in the "corn belt" of the Midwest, where in his childhood he knew the sea only by listening to a conch shell souvenir from Florida. When World War II took him to the sea for the first time, he plunged in for a swim and within five minutes was wrapped in the stinging tentacles of a Portuguese man-o-war. This was the beginning of his study of all dangerous animals of the sea, a course that turned him into a professional zoologist as well.